SO-CJM-305

Grades
K–1

Think, Do and Read
Mini-Books

By
Dona L. Lynch

**Cover illustration by
Julie Anderson**

**Inside illustrations by
Ann Lutnicki**

Publishers
Instructional Fair • TS Denison
Grand Rapids, Michigan 49544

INSTRUCTIONAL FAIR • TS DENISON

Instructional Fair • TS Denison grants the right to the individual purchaser to reproduce the student activity materials in this book for noncommercial individual or classroom use only. Reproduction for an entire school or school system is strictly prohibited. No part of this publication may be reproduced for storage in a retrieval system, or transmitted in any form or by any means, electronic, mechanical, recording, or otherwise, without the prior written permission of the publisher. For information regarding permission write to:
Instructional Fair • TS Denison, P.O. Box 1650, Grand Rapids, MI 49501.

Credits
Author: Dona L. Lynch
Cover Illustration: Julie Anderson
Inside Illustrations: Ann Lutnicki
Project Director & Editor:
    Debra Olson Pressnall
Art Production: Julie Anderson
Typesetting: Deborah McNiff

About the Author
Dona Lynch lives in Trumansburg, a rural town in New York, and teaches kindergarten in Enfield Elementary School. Although her family graciously allows her a small room to store her educational materials, their house is littered with ideas for new stories and activities. Her daughter, Rachael, usually helps staple the books together and her husband, Tim, puts up with a cluttered dining room table. Bob, their cat, just watches the production. Her son, Eric, used to be involved in these activities too, but he's grown up now and lives away from home. When she is not teaching, she enjoys two-stepping to Cajun/Zydeco music, hiking in the Adirondack Mountains, and almost every day after school, no matter what the season, walking with her best friend. It is often during these times that she thinks of new ideas for other *Think, Do and Read* booklets.

Standard Book Number: 1-56822-530-X
Think, Do and Read Mini-Books
Copyright © 1997 by Instructional Fair • TS Denison
2400 Turner Avenue NW
Grand Rapids, Michigan 49544

All Rights Reserved • Printed in the USA

Dear Colleague,

   Are you a kindergarten or first grade teacher looking for a way to incorporate specific skill instruction with literacy experiences? Do you find that every time you purchase an activity book for Grades K-3, you are given some great project ideas for your second and third grade colleagues but the ideas are too advanced for your students? If you have answered "yes" to either of the above questions, this book is for you! Leaf through the pages and you find 25 fun, skill-based Think, Do and Read Mini-Books. THINK because your students will need to remember or be taught new skills, use the visual clues to help with the text, and in some cases, decide on a final sentence. DO because your students will be cutting, pasting, coloring, and/or writing. READ because your students will be able to read the booklets independently.

   All of these mini-books have been tested with my kindergarten classes. I have observed how my five- and six-year-old students easily understood the material in the booklets. Before my students take their booklets home, they often practice reading them to each other, to friends in different grades, or to various staff members. Parents have told me that not only do their children read the booklets to their brothers and sisters but to family pets as well.

   Depending on the abilities of your students, just photocopy the pattern pages or modify them to meet the needs of your students. For example, in booklets where the focus is on whole words and the students are not ready for that concept, I print the endings of the words and have the children concentrate on beginning sounds. Also, depending on the ability of my class, I have some students whose only job is to color and/or cut and glue the pictures to the pages. Every mini-book can be adapted for your classroom or for individual students.

   In my classroom, I begin the school year with the mini-books "Shapes," "Insects," and "People in Our Classroom." Near the end of the school year my students complete the mini-book "The Little _____ Seed." As a result, the booklets are listed in the order that they are used in my classroom. The titles are self-explanatory and reflect a general unit of study; math and science concepts are incorporated into many themes. Perhaps you might be interested in mini-books about animals? Look for "Mammals" or "Who Made These Tracks?" I would be happy to hear how you are using this resource, *Think, Do and Read Mini-Books* in your classroom.

                                   Have a great year and keep reading!

                                   Dona Lynch

Table of Contents

Instructions for Mini-Books

Note: Please be sure to read the specific instructions for the selected mini-book before making photocopies of the pages. This is important to remember because some mini-book pages need to be photocopied back to back. Also note: Children may need to spend more than one class session to complete the work. You might wish to provide pocket folders for the children to store their work.

SHAPES
(Patterns on pages 9–13)

Preparation
- Use the patterns on the pattern page (page 13) for making construction paper shapes. (The number and color of each shape is indicated on the HELPING PAGE.) Additional shapes are needed for page 7. Precut the shapes for the children to use when completing the work.

Directions
Teacher
- Staple each mini-book along the left edge after the work is completed.

Students
- Paste the corresponding shapes on the pages.
- Fill in the blanks to complete the sentences. Refer to the HELPING PAGE.
- For page 6 cut out the shapes and complete the sentence.
- For page 7 use the shapes to make an object and then complete the sentence.
- Cut apart the pages and then assemble the mini-book.

INSECTS
(Patterns on pages 14–16)

Directions
Students
- Cut apart the pages and then assemble the mini-books.
- Fill in the blanks to complete the sentences. Answers: page 1, six; page 2, three; page 3, two; page 4, ant; and page 5, answers may vary.

PEOPLE IN OUR CLASSROOM
(Patterns on pages 17–21)

Preparation
- Photograph each student and yourself individually.
- To prepare a booklet page for each student, photocopy enough copies of page 18 for your class.
- On the individual student pages, tape in place each student's photograph and your photograph inside the frames.
- Write the students' names on the respective HELPING PAGES. Make additional name boxes if needed.
- Number the individual student photographs to correspond with the HELPING PAGES. *Note:* Be sure to write the number inside the box on each photograph page. The numbers will be covered when the names of the students are pasted on the mini-book pages.
- Make enough photocopies of each photograph page and HELPING PAGE for students to individually make a mini-book.
- The mini-book pages can be photocopied back to back.

Directions
Teacher
- Read the students' names on the HELPING PAGES with the your students.
- Fold the pages on the solid black line and assemble the mini-books. (If appropriate, allow the students to assemble the mini-books.) Staple each mini-book on the left edge before the work is completed.

Students
- Cut out the names and paste them on the corresponding pages in the mini-book.
- Draw a picture on the last page of the mini-book.

MY FIVE SENSES
(Patterns on pages 22-26)

Preparation
- *Note:* Photocopy the following pages back to back: pages 22 and 23, and pages 24 and 25.
- Fold the pages in half and staple the mini-book on the left edge of the cover before the work is completed.
- Gather magazines for the children to use for finding pictures of objects.

Directions
Students
- Clip pictures of objects and have an adult record the names on the HELPING PAGE.
- Paste the objects on the corresponding pages and print the names in the sentences.

WORMS IN APPLES
(Patterns on pages 27–31)

Directions
Students
- To make an accordion-folded book, paste the following pages together (covering the copyright line):
  → paste the top edge of page 27 to the bottom of page 28
  → paste the top edge of page 28 to the bottom of page 29
  → paste the top edge of page 29 to the bottom of page 30
  → paste the top edge of page 30 to the bottom of page 31
- Fold the booklet pages on the dotted lines.
- Color the apples and worms.
- Count the worms and print the corresponding numeral in the blank space. Finish the sentence on page 8.

FLOATING DOWN
(Patterns on pages 32–38)

Directions
Teacher
- Staple the mini-book pages on the copyright lines before the work is completed.

Students
- Assemble the mini-books.
- Trace the path of each leaf and over the lightened words.
- Color the leaves with the corresponding colors.
- Complete the sentence on page 38.

AUTUMN LEAVES
(Patterns on pages 39–41)

Preparation
- Encourage the students to collect leaves and press them before taping them in the mini-books.
- Decide how many photocopies will be needed of each page shown on pattern page 40. Cut apart the pages.
- If appropriate, provide a folder for each student to use while completing the work.

Directions
Teacher
- Help the students identify their leaves.
- Staple each mini-book when the work is completed.

Student
- Select the appropriate page for each leaf in the collection.
- Tape each leaf to a page. Use wide clear adhesive tape.
- Fill in the blanks to complete the sentences. On the last page of the mini-book, finish the sentence with an idea about what can be done with leaves and draw a picture to illustrate it.
- Assemble the mini-book when the work is finished.

HALLOWEEN TREATS
(Patterns on pages 42–48)

Preparation
- To assemble the booklet, photocopy pattern page 43 on the back of page 42, continue by copying page 48 on the back of pages 44–47. Make one additional copy of page 48. (There must be five copies of page 48 in each mini-book.)
- Assemble the mini-book by showing a fence pattern page alongside the page that shows children standing at the door. Staple the pages together on the left edge of the cover.
- Cut out construction paper flaps to fit on pattern page 48. The flaps hide the treats that are glued on these pages.
- Collect magazines for pictures of treats.

Directions
Student
- Read the text and decide how many treats are given to each group of children.
- Fill in the blanks to complete the sentences.
- Glue a flap above the fence to hide the treat. (Five flaps will be glued.)
- Cut out the treats. Read the text and then paste the corresponding number of treats under each flap. Print the numeral on the flap.

FIVE FAT TURKEYS
(Patterns on pages 49–52)

Preparation
- Photocopy pattern pages 50 and 51 back to back.
- Fold the pattern pages in half on the solid black line and assemble the mini-book.
- Staple the pages together on the left edge of the cover.
- Photocopy the HELPING PAGE. Cut the pattern page in half and give to each student the pictures of five turkeys and one cook.

Directions
Student
- Print the initial consonants in the title.
- Fill in the blanks with the word "we."
- Cut out the turkeys and the cook.
- Paste five turkeys on page 1 and the cook on page 3.

OPPOSITES
(Patterns on pages 53–57)

Preparation
- Photocopy the following pattern pages back to back: pages 53 and 54, pages 55 and 56.
- To assemble the booklet, cut apart the pages on the dashed lines. Fold the smaller pages on the solid lines. Assemble the pages in order and staple them together on the left edge of the cover.

Directions
Student
- Fill in the blanks. Refer to the HELPING PAGE.
- Color the pictures.
- On pages 13 and 14 write another pair of opposite words and draw pictures to illustrate them.

NOCTURNAL
(Patterns on pages 58–68)

Preparation
- Photocopy the following pattern pages back to back: 59 and 60, 61 and 62, 63 and 64, 65 and 66. Photocopy the mini-book cover on separate paper. Provide an additional sheet of paper for the back cover of the book.
- Assemble the pages and staple them together on the left edge of the cover.

Directions
Student
- Read the text and fill in the blanks. Refer to the HELPING PAGES for the spelling of the words.
- Cut out the pictures of the animals from the HELPING PAGES and paste them in the corresponding scenes.

PHASES OF THE MOON
(Patterns on pages 69–73)

Directions
Student
- Cut apart the mini-book pages on the dashed lines.
- Assemble the pages and staple them together on the left edge of the cover.
- Fill in the blanks to complete the sentences. Refer to the HELPING PAGE for the spelling of the words.

WHO MADE THESE TRACKS?
(Patterns on pages 74–80)

Preparation
- Make four copies of flap A and B (on pattern page 74) for each mini-book.

Directions
Teacher
- Staple the pages of the mini-book before the work is completed.

Student
- Fill in the blanks to complete the sentences. Refer to the HELPING PAGE for the spelling of the words.
- Clip pictures of animals and paste them on the corresponding pages. Be sure to paste each animal on the large "X". Use the HELPING PAGE for identifying the tracks.
- Place flap A or B on each story page by stapling or pasting it to the right edge of the page. (The flap will hide the animal or person that makes the tracks.)
- Cut apart the pages on the dashed lines and assemble them into a mini-book.

WINTER CLOTHES
(Patterns on pages 81–83)

Directions
Student
- Cut apart the pages on the dashed lines and assemble them into a mini-book.
- Decide which page 6 to keep in the booklet: mittens or gloves.
- Staple the pages together on the left edge of the cover.
- Fill in the blanks to complete the sentences. Use the HELPING PAGE for the correct spelling of the missing words.
- Finish the sentence on page 7.

COMMUNITY HELPERS
(Patterns on pages 84–93)

Preparation
- Each community helper page will have a flap that hides the worker. Make five photocopies of pattern page 90 for each mini-book.

Directions
Teacher
- Staple the booklets after the work is completed.

Student
- Prepare the flap for each story page. Trim the pattern page by cutting on the dashed line. Fold the page in half and glue or staple the sections together to make a flap. Glue or staple the flap on the right edge of the story page. Repeat the steps to prepare the remaining flaps.
- Cut out the pictures (pages 91–93) to complete the sentences. Paste them on the story pages and fill in the blanks to complete the sentences on the back of the flaps. Use the HELPING PAGE to identify each community helper.

IS THIS MY VALENTINE?
(Patterns on pages 94–100)

Preparation
- This mini-book can be made very special by using construction paper or wallpaper samples for the covers. Students may wish to decorate their covers with construction paper hearts. Use pattern page 94 as the title page of the mini-book or duplicate it on construction paper.
- Gather various craft materials and construction paper for students to use when making valentines for the mini-books.

Directions
Teacher
- Staple the mini-book pages together on the top edge of the cover.

Student
- Print missing words to complete the sentences. Note: The same sentence is repeated four times on the page.
- Cut valentine pictures from the HELPING PAGE and tape or paste them on the story page.
- Print "yes" or "no" underneath each flap to answer the question. Look carefully at the valentine picture (flap) before writing the answer.
- On page 5 make a valentine from various craft materials and finish the sentence.
- Assemble the pages when the work is completed.

WHERE DO YOU LIVE?
(Patterns on pages 101–108)

Preparation
- Prepare a photograph of each student in the classroom. You may wish to use the same photographs that are used for the mini-book, "People in Our Classroom."
- Make five photocopies of the child's photograph for the mini-book. *Note:* Each child will have a personalized mini-book when it is completed.
- Make five photocopies of page 107 or 108 for each child.

Directions
Student
- Assemble pages and staple them together on the left edge of the cover.
- Cut out copies of photograph and paste them near the right corner of each story page.
- Trace or copy the sentence on the speech bubble and paste it near the photograph.
- On page 5 draw a picture of his/her own home and paste the corresponding speech bubble on the page.

WAYS TO GO
(Patterns on pages 109–118)

Preparation
- Photocopy pattern page 109 (mini-book cover) on construction paper. Photocopy the remaining pages on copier paper.

Directions
Student
- Fold each story page in half on the solid black lines. Be sure the pictures can be seen when folding the paper.
- Cut two slits in the paper to make a tab as shown. (Cut on the dashed lines.)
- Fold the paper tab forward to make a new crease.
- Open the paper and push the paper tab to make it look like the example shown.
- Repeat the steps for other pop-up pages.
- Glue the pages together as shown.
- Print the first letter of each word in the sentences. Use the HELPING PAGE for guidance.
- Cut out the vehicle and paste it on the corresponding paper tab.
- For page 7 draw a mode of transportation on a separate piece of paper and complete the sentence on the page. Cut out the illustration and paste it on the tab.

GOING TO AN ISLAND
(Patterns on pages 119–124)

Directions
Student

- Cut apart the pages on the dashed lines.
- Assemble the pages and staple them together on the left edge of the cover. (Place staples on the copyright line area.)
- Fill in the blanks to complete the sentences. Use the HELPING PAGE for correct spelling of words.
- On page 123 complete the sentences and illustrate the chosen answers.

THE KOALA
(Patterns on pages 125–130)

Directions
Student

- Assemble the pages and staple them together on the left edge of the cover.
- Cut out pictures from pattern page 130 and paste them over the corresponding numbers.

LOOKING FOR MAMMALS
(Patterns on pages 131–148)

Preparation

- To make this mini-book, photocopy the pages back to back. The mini-book ends with page 17 which is blank on the backside.
- Preassemble the mini-book for the student. Staple the pages together on the left edge of the cover.

Directions
Student

- Fill in the blanks to complete the sentences. Use the HELPING PAGE for the correct spelling of the words.
- On pages 16 and 17 paste pictures from the patterns on the HELPING PAGE. Draw some scenery for each animal.

AMPHIBIANS
(Patterns on pages 149–153)

Directions
Student

- Cut apart the pages on the dashed lines.
- Assemble the pages and staple them together on the left edge of the cover.
- Set aside the HELPING PAGE for reference when pasting pictures of animals on the story pages.
- Cut out the pictures of the animals (pattern page 153) and paste them on the pages.

THE LITTLE SEED
(Patterns on pages 154–168)

Preparation

- Photocopy the pages of the mini-book back to back. Start with pattern page 154 and print page 155 on the back of it. The mini-book ends on page 15 (pattern page 168) which is blank on the backside.
- Collect wallpaper samples for the mini-book covers. Use pattern page 154 as the title page of the mini-book.
- Provide brown, yellow and blue construction paper for the earth, sun, and rain.
- Supply flower seeds for the mini-books. Select a flower seed that is large in size (e.g. marigold, aster, nasturtium, cosmos). Save the packet for the children to see.

Directions
Teacher

- To make picture cards (HELPING CARDS), print the words "sun," "earth," and "rain" on large cards. Glue brown construction paper near the word "earth." Glue a yellow construction paper sun near the word "sun" and blue raindrops near the word "rain."

Student

- Print the name of the seed on the cover and the title page of the mini-book.
- Fill in the blanks to complete the sentences. Look at the HELPING CARDS for the correct spelling of the words.
- Glue pieces of torn construction paper to make the earth, rain, and sun on the story pages.
- Glue real seeds on pages 2–8.
- Glue pieces of green construction paper to show the flower growing and in full bloom on pages 10–13.
- On page 15 print words that people might say in response to "thank you."

Variation

- To make a very special mini-book with torn construction paper (similar technique used by Eric Carle), photocopy only the text of this mini-book on copier paper. To make the pages smaller, fit two mini-book pages on one sheet of copier paper. Label the pages with the words "sun," "earth," and "rain." Encourage the child to use torn construction paper to illustrate each page. This project will take several class sessions. This book is a beautiful when finished!

THE MEAT EATER IS COMING!
(Patterns on pages 169–176)

Directions
Teacher

- To make picture cards (HELPING CARDS), print the names of the dinosaurs on large cards. Also include pictures from the HELPING PAGE on the cards.

Student

- Assemble the pages. Add a blank page at the end of the mini-book and label it page 7.
- Staple the pages together on the left edge of the cover.
- Fill in the blanks to complete the words. Use the HELPING CARDS for the correct spelling of the words.
- Cut out the pictures of the dinosaurs and paste them on the corresponding pages.
- On page 7 write what happens when corythosaurus meets tyrannosaurus. Draw a picture to illustrate the sentence.

Shapes

By

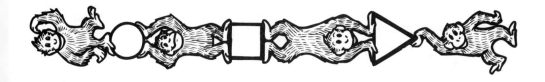

Here is one
ellipse.

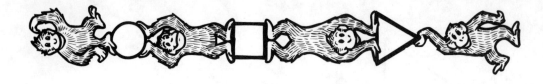

Here are ____ ____ ____

three

rectangles.

3

Here are two

circles.

____ ____ ____

2

© Instructional Fair • TS Denison

IF21840 *Think, Do & Read*

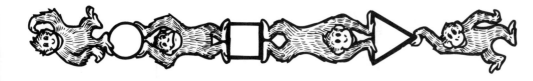

Here are five

_ _ _ _

squares.

4

Here are

four _ _ _ _

triangles.

I can make ____
with shapes.

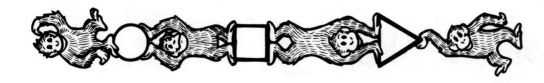

Here are six ____.

Shapes

1 ⬭ red

2 ◯ ◯ pink

3 ▭ ▭ ▭ green

4 △ △ △ △ blue

5 ◻ ◻ ◻ ◻ ◻ yellow

- -

Patterns

Insects

By

Insects have ___ legs.

1

Insects have _ _ _ _ _
body parts.

2

Insects have _ _ _ antennae.

3

This is an insect.

It is an ___.

4

Insects can

5

People in Our Classroom

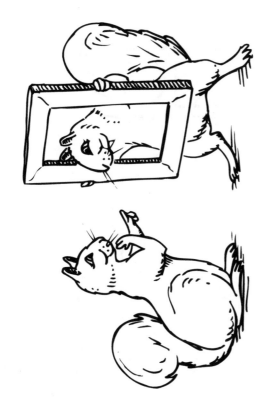

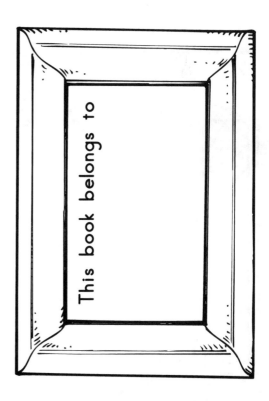

This book belongs to

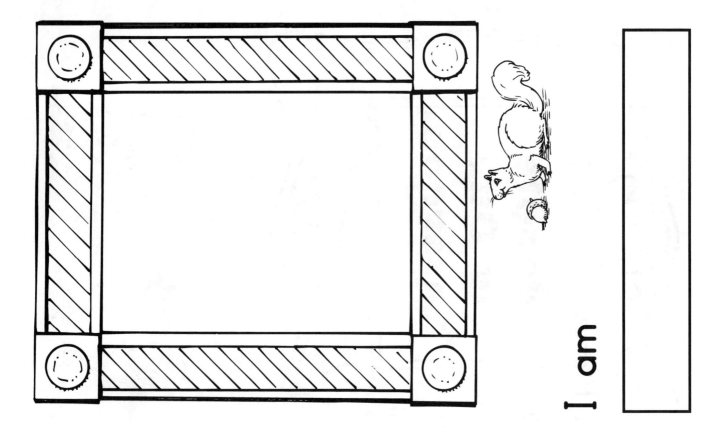

I am

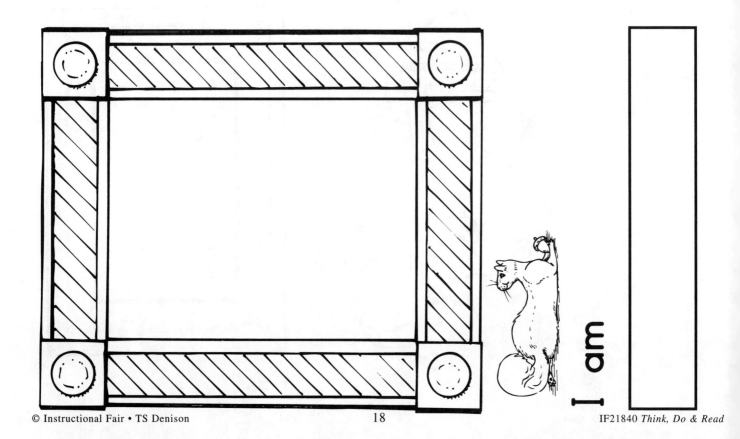

I am

Hooray for our class!

I am

People in Our Classroom
The Girls

1

3

5

7

9

11

12

13

15

18

People in Our Classroom
The Boys

2

4

6

8

10

14

16

17

19

20

My Five Senses

By

My five senses
can help me
learn about my
environment.

6

I can touch

with my

I can taste

with my

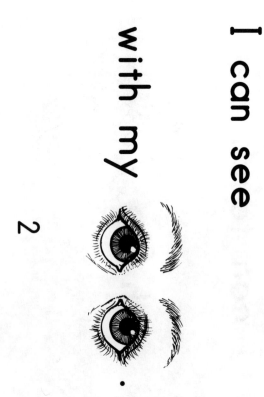

.

5

I can see

with my

.

2

I can smell

with my 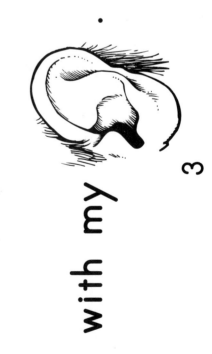 .

4

I can hear

with my .

3

My Five Senses

Do I have pictures for:

hear

see

touch

taste

smell

?   Yes!

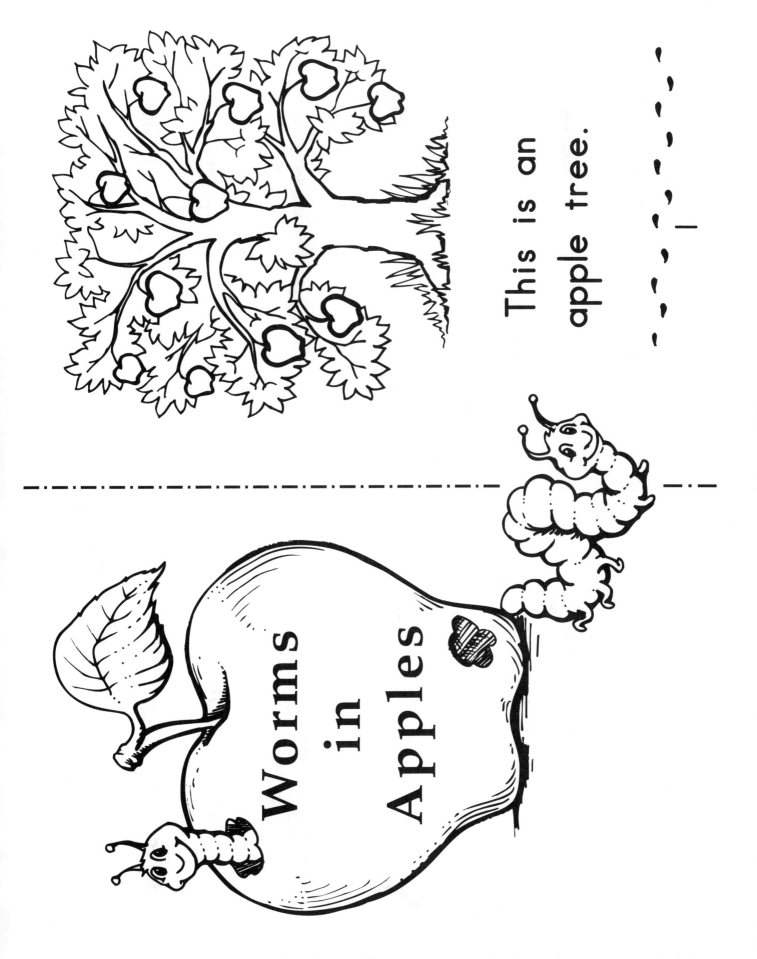

This is an apple tree.

Worms in Apples

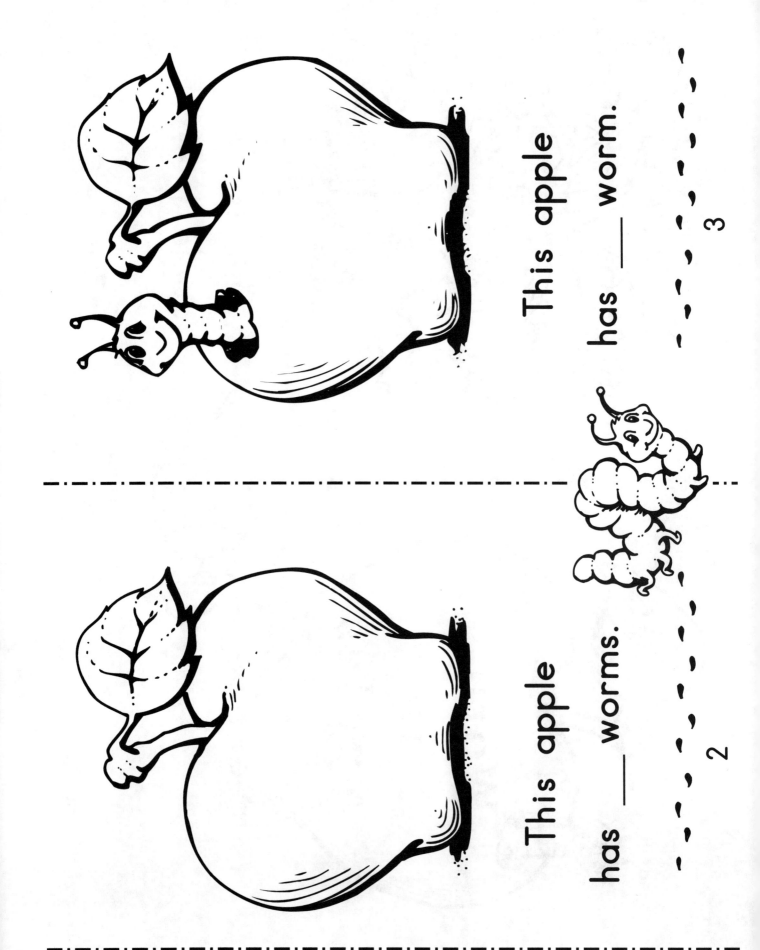

This apple

has ___ worm.

3

This apple

has ___ worms.

2

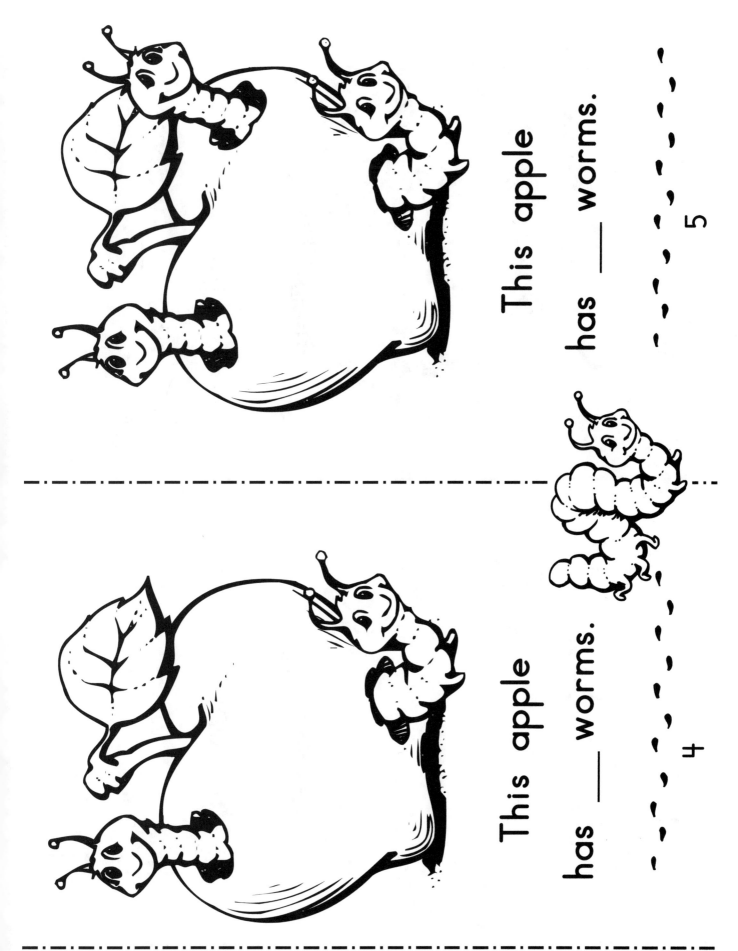

This apple

has ___ worms.

5

This apple

has ___ worms.

4

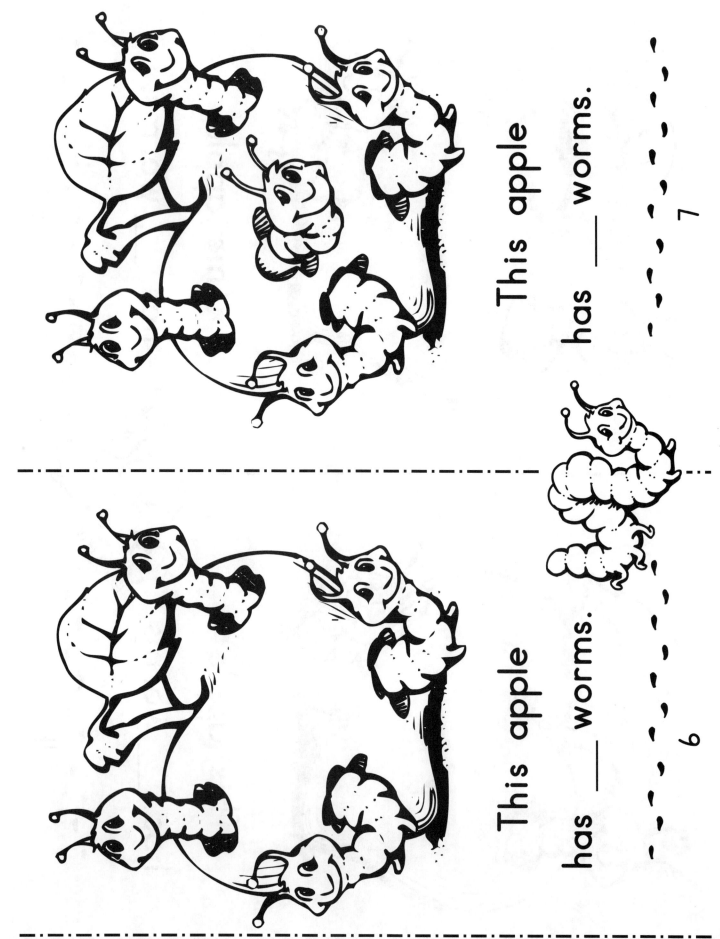

This apple

has ___ worms.

7

This apple

has ___ worms.

6

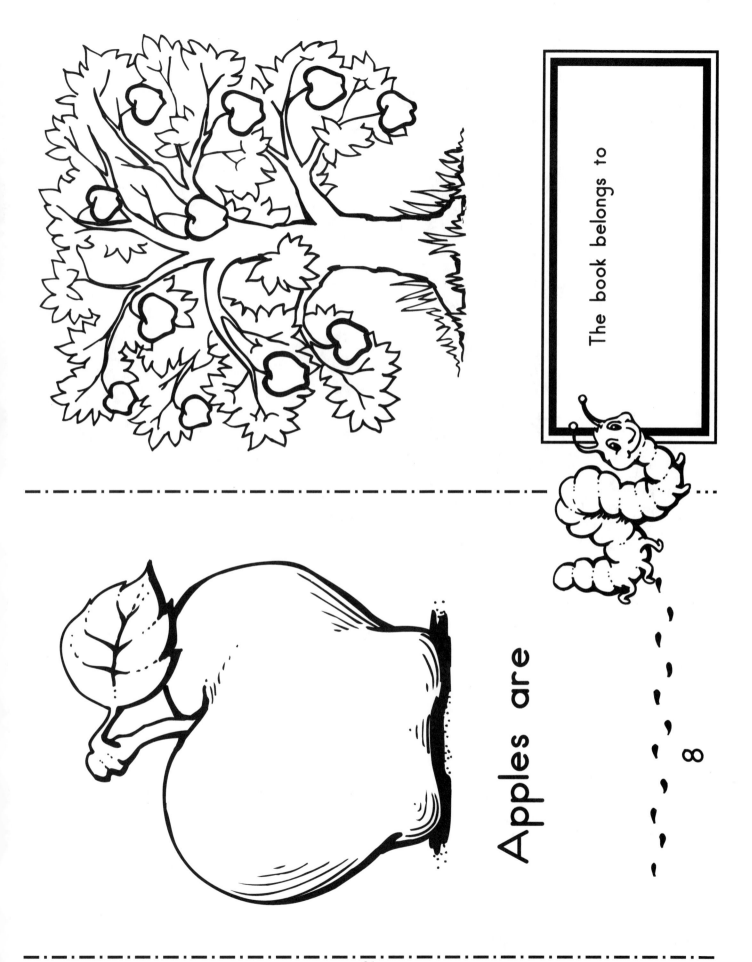

The book belongs to

Apples are

8

Floating Down

By

© Instructional Fair • TS Denison

IF21840 *Think, Do & Read*

Here comes an orange leaf,

Gently floating down.

1

© Instructional Fair • TS Denison

IF21840 *Think, Do & Read*

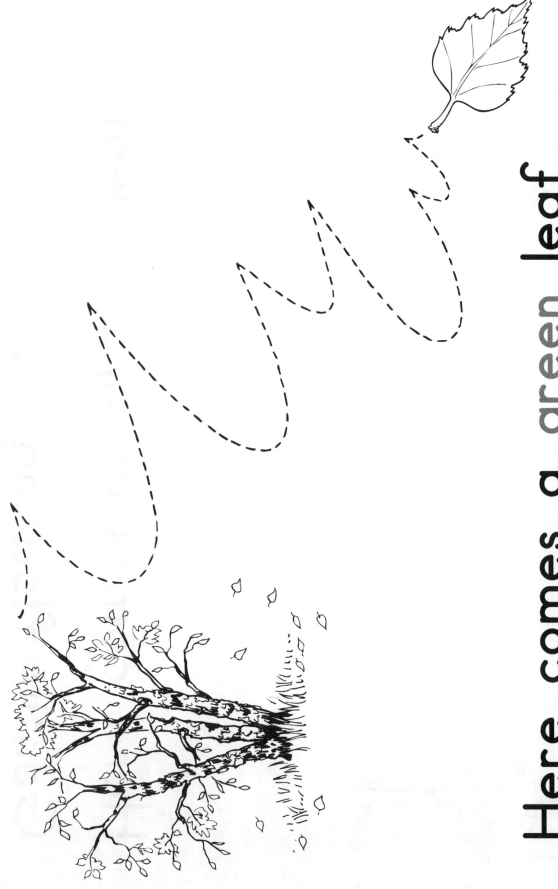

Here comes a green leaf,
Gently floating down.

Here comes a red leaf,

Gently floating down.

3

Here comes a brown leaf,

Gently floating down.

4

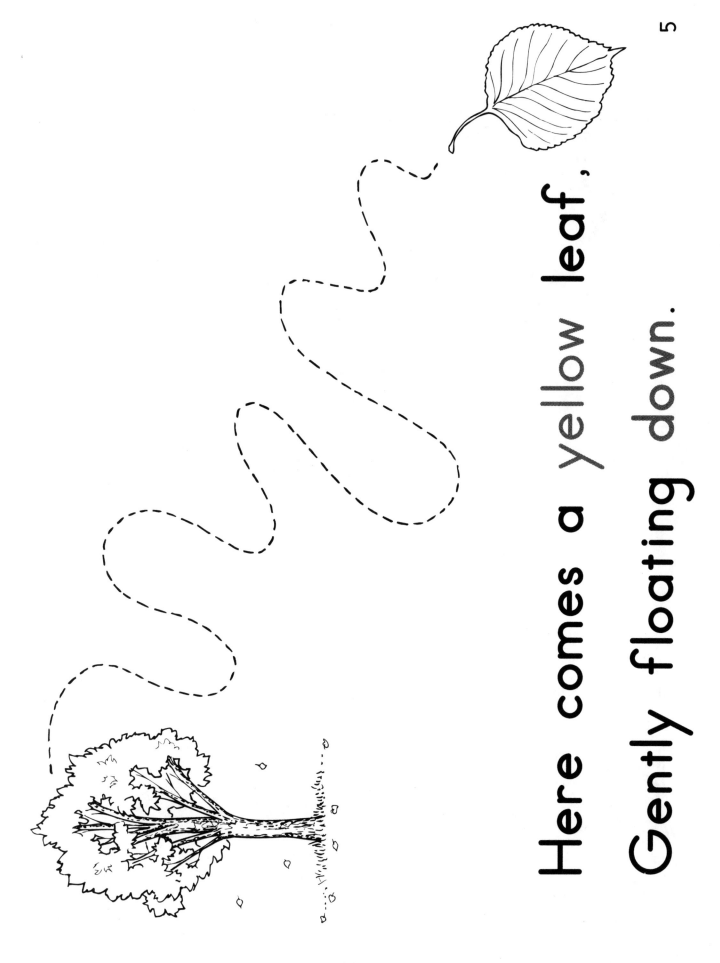

5

Here comes a yellow leaf,
Gently floating down.

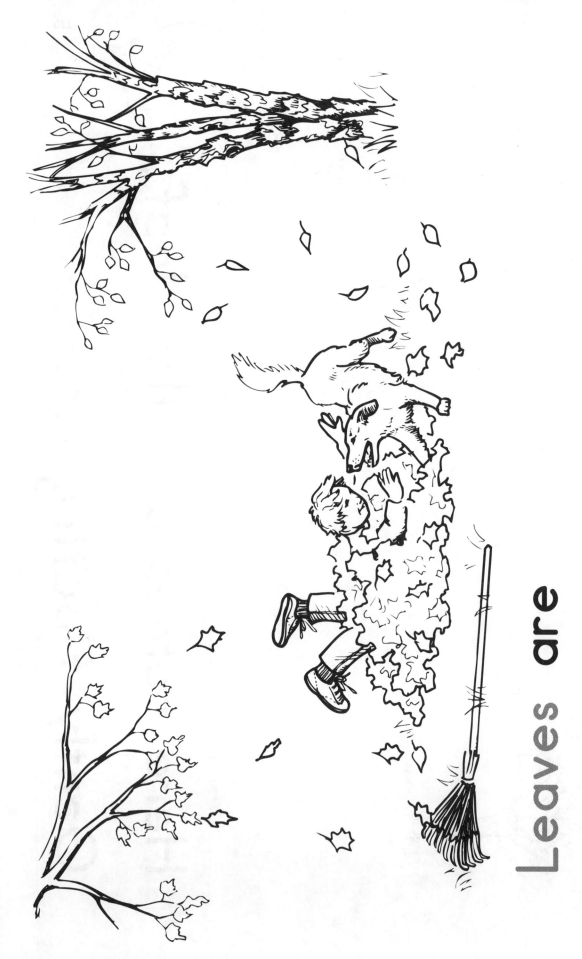

Leaves are

© Instructional Fair • TS Denison

IF21840 *Think, Do & Read*

Autumn Leaves

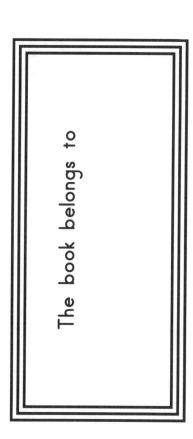

The book belongs to

This is a

leaf.

_____

This is an

leaf.

_____

I like to

This is my
favorite leaf.

Halloween Treats

By

Trick or treat.

Trick or treat.

Please give me

___ good thing

to eat.

Trick or treat.

Trick or treat.

Please give us

___ good things

to eat.

Trick or treat.

Trick or treat.

Please give us

_ _ _ _ _ good things

to eat.

Trick or treat.

Trick or treat.

Please give us

_ _ _ _ good things

to eat.

Trick or treat.

Trick or treat.

Please give us
____ good things
to eat.

Glue flap here.

ive _at

_urkeys

_

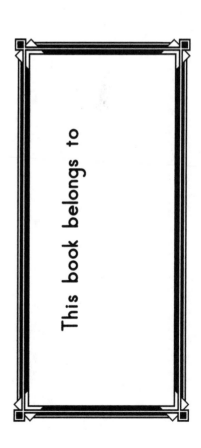

This book belongs to

So, that's why we're
here you see!

4

Five fat turkeys
are ___ .

1

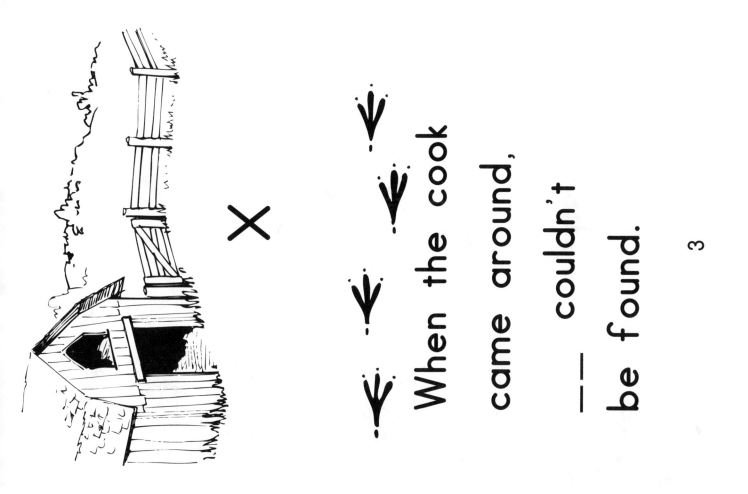

X

When the cook
came around,
___ couldn't
be found.

3

___ slept all
night in a tree.

2

Five Fat Turkeys

Opposites

By

13

© Instructional Fair • TS Denison

2

— —

1

———————

14

— —

3

— — — — — —

12

© Instructional Fair • TS Denison

IF21840 *Think, Do & Re*

— — — — —

5

— — — — —

10

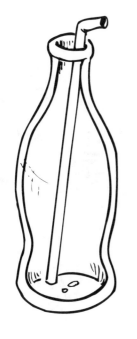

— — — — —

7

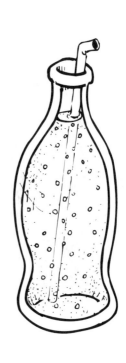

— — — —

8

— — —

II

— — —

4

— — —

9

— — —

6

© Instructional Fair • TS Denison

IF21840 *Think, Do & Read*

Opposites

up

sad

in

little

day

down

full

night

happy

out

big

empty

© Instructional Fair • TS Denison

IF21840 *Think, Do & Read*

We Are Nocturnal

By

A ___ is a
nocturnal animal.
A bat is awake at
_ _ _ _ _ .

1

An _ _ _ _ _ _ is a

nocturnal animal.

An opossum is awake at

2 _ _ _ _ _ .

A _____ _____

is a nocturnal animal.

A flying squirrel is

awake at _____.

3

A _ _ _ _ _ is a
nocturnal animal.
A skunk is awake at
_ _ _ _ _ .

A _ _ _ _ is a
nocturnal animal.
A moth is awake at
_ _ _ _ _.

5

A _ _ _ _ _ _ _ is a
nocturnal animal.
A raccoon is awake at
_ _ _ _ _ .

An _ _ _ is a
nocturnal animal.
An owl is awake at
_ _ _ _ _ .

7

A _____ is a
nocturnal animal.
A bullfrog is awake at
8 _____ .

We Are Nocturnal

Nocturnal animals are awake at <u>night</u>.

1 bat

4 skunk

2 opossum

3 flying squirrel

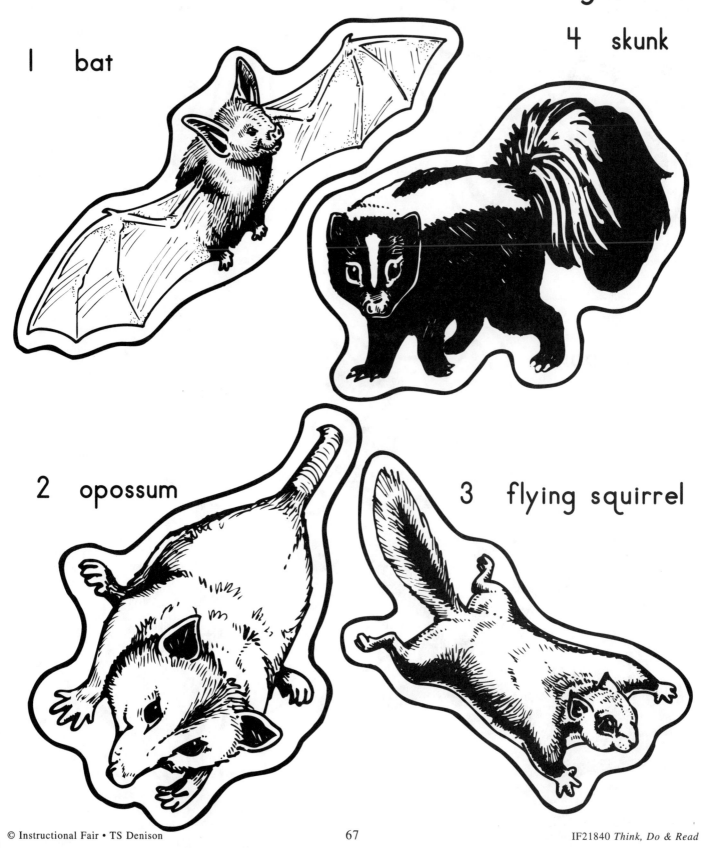

© Instructional Fair • TS Denison

IF21840 *Think, Do & Read*

5 moth

8 bullfrog

6 raccoon

7 owl

Phases of the Moon

This book belongs to

This is the

_ _ _ _ _
phase of the
waxing moon.

2

This is the

_ _ _ _ moon.

_ _
1

This is the _____ moon.

4

This is the _____ phase of the waxing moon.

3

This is the

_ _ _ _

phase of the

waning moon.

6

This is the

_ _ _ _

phase of the

waning moon.

5

© Instructional Fair • TS Denison

IF21840 *Think, Do & Read*

Phases of the Moon

1 <u>new</u> moon

2 <u>crescent</u> phase

3 <u>gibbous</u> phase

4 <u>full</u> moon

5 <u>gibbous</u> phase

6 <u>crescent</u> phase

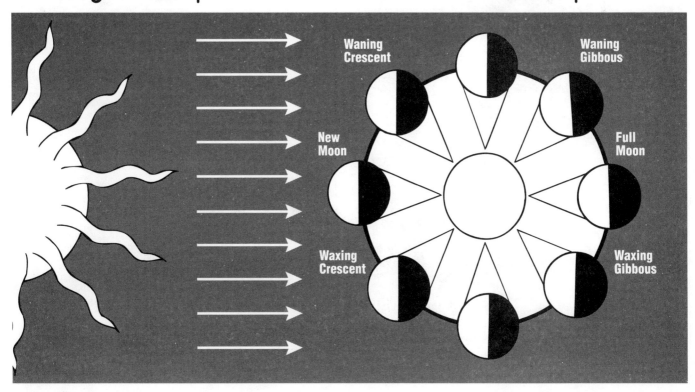

Flap B   Need 4 copies.

Who Made These Tracks?

Flap A   Need 4 copies.

These tracks were made by a . . . . __ __ __ __ . **1**

These tracks were made by a . . . . __ __ __ __ . **2**

X

These tracks were made by a . . . .

3

X

These tracks were made by a . . . .

4

X

These tracks were made by a . . .

— — — — .

5

X

These tracks were made by a . . .

— — — — .

6

These tracks were made by a . . . _____ 7

×

These tracks were made by a . . . _____ 8

×

© Instructional Fair • TS Denison

IF21840 *Think, Do & Read*

Pictures for
Who Made These Tracks?

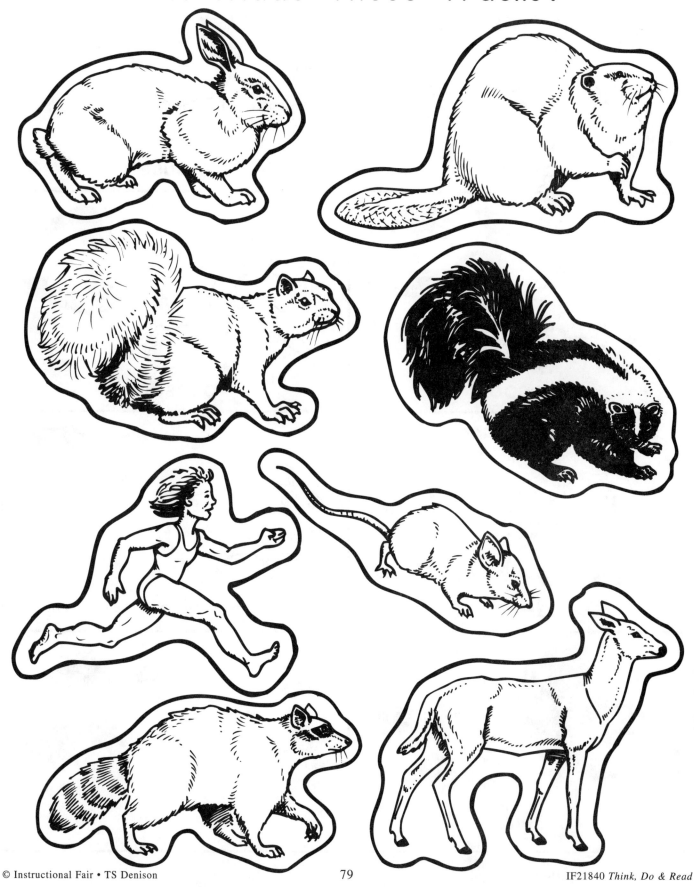

Who Made These Tracks?

squirrel

mouse

raccoon

person

deer

rabbit

skunk

beaver

Clothes

___ ___

I put on my ___ ___

1 .

I put on my ___

2 .

This book belongs to

© Instructional Fair • TS Denison

IF21840 *Think, Do & Read*

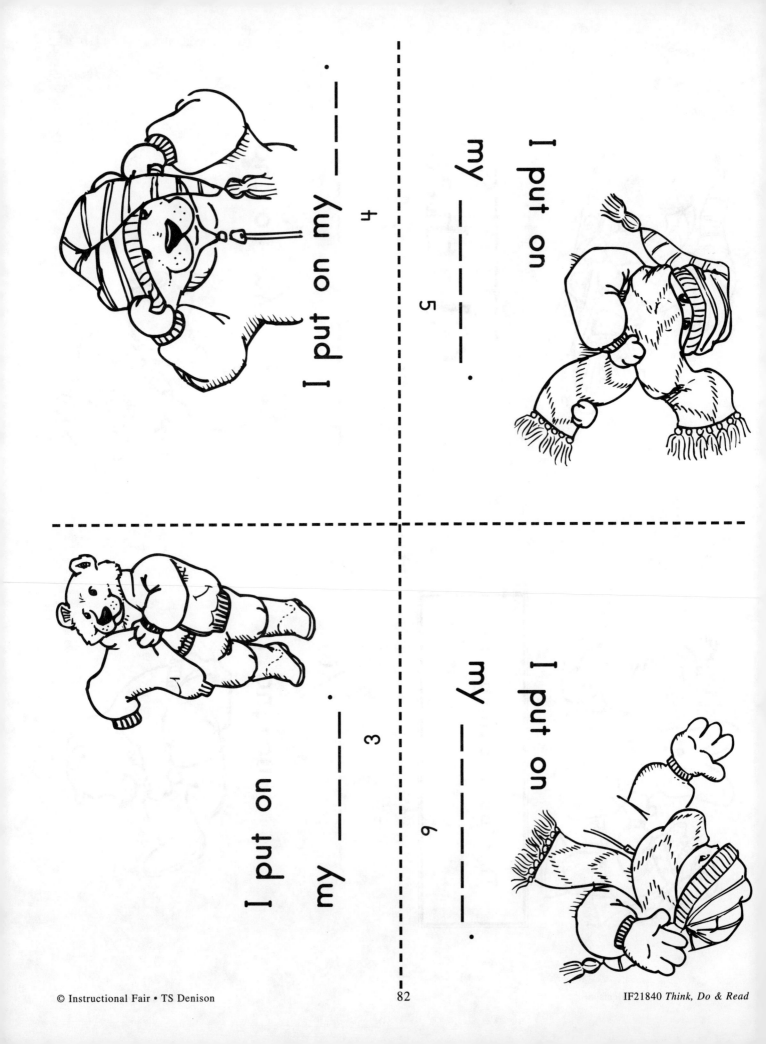

I put on my __ __ __ __ .
4

I put on my __ __ __ __ .
5

I put on my __ __ __ __ .
3

I put on my __ __ __ __ .
6

© Instructional Fair • TS Denison
IF21840 *Think, Do & Read*

Winter Clothes

gloves

mittens

scarf

boots

hat

coat

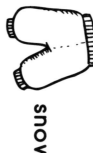
snow pants

Now I can

7

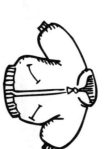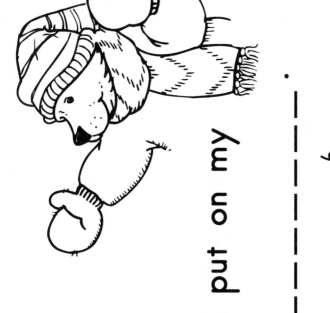

I put on my _ _ _ _ .

6

© Instructional Fair • TS Denison

IF21840 *Think, Do & Read*

Community Helpers

CHATEAU CAFE

Fire House No. I

MAIL

Post Office

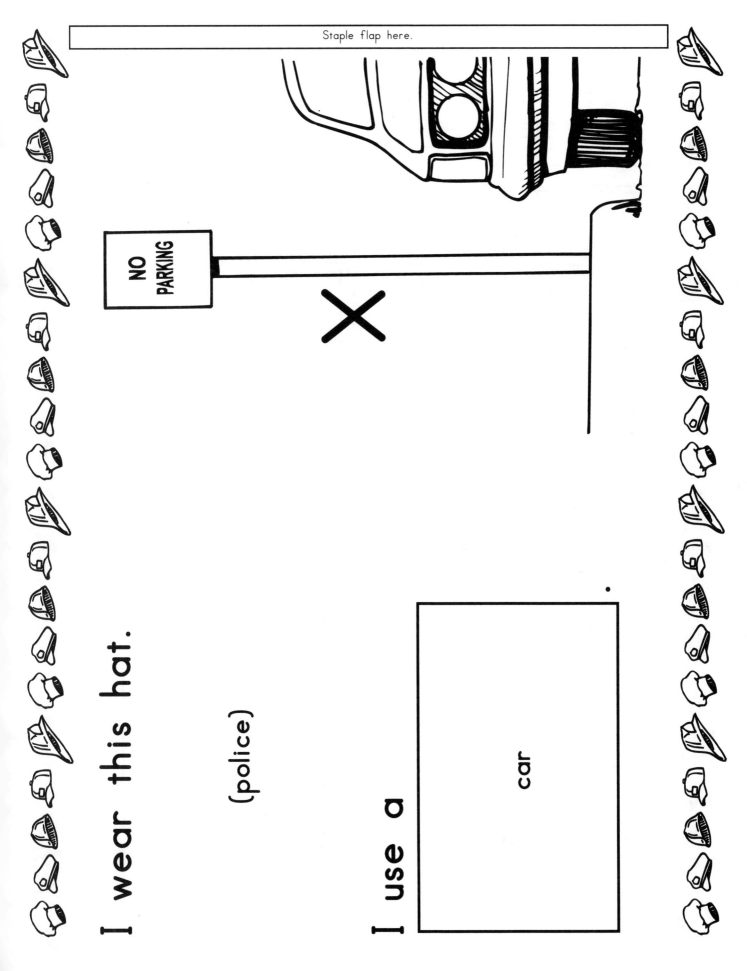

NO PARKING

I wear this hat.

(police)

I use a

car

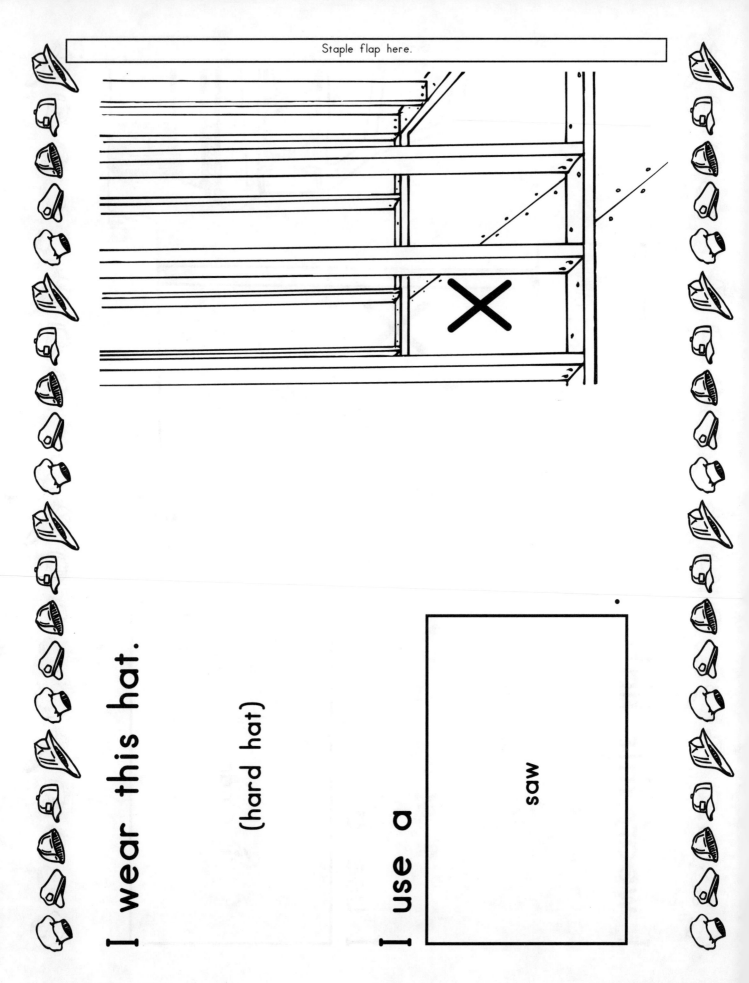

I wear this hat.

(hard hat)

I use a

saw

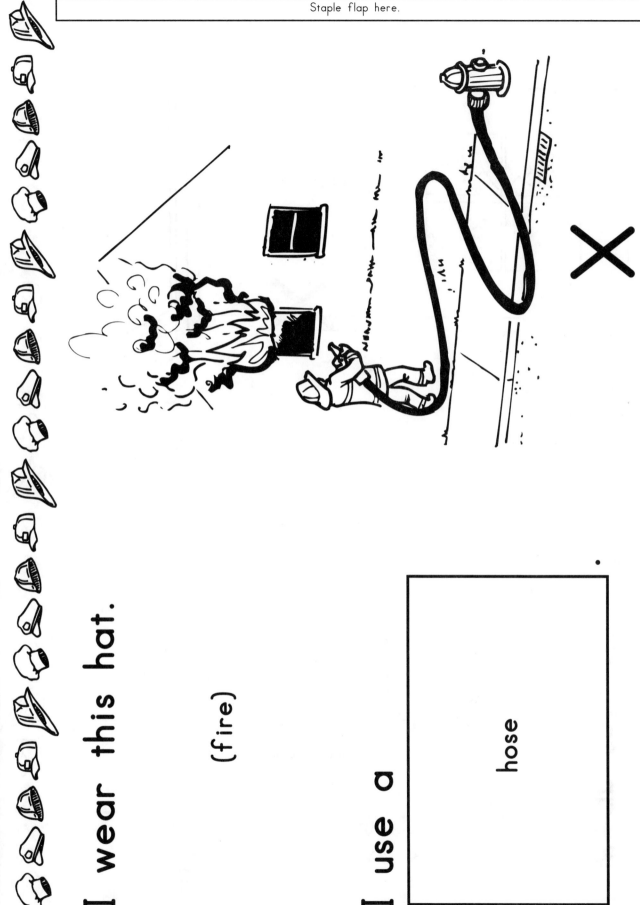

I wear this hat.

(fire)

I use a

hose

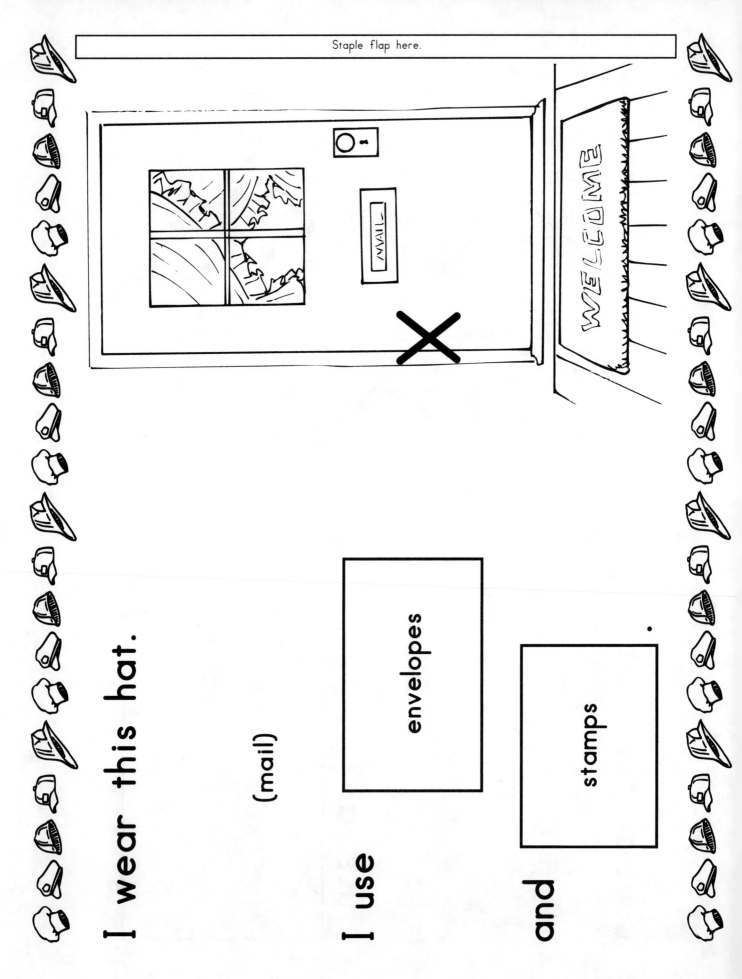

I wear this hat.

(mail)

I use

envelopes

and

stamps

WELCOME

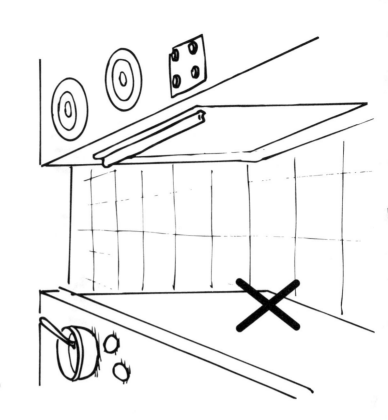
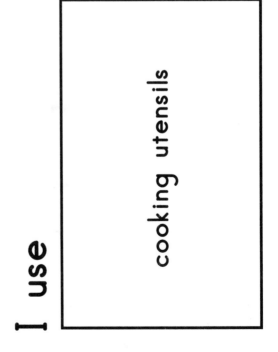

I wear this hat.

(chef)

I use

cooking utensils

Who am I?

I am a

_____ .

Pictures for Community Helpers

Hats to Wear

mail

fire

hard hat

chef

police

Things to Use

envelope

stamps

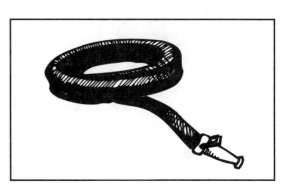

hose

saw

Pictures for Community Helpers

Things to Use

cooking utensils

car

People

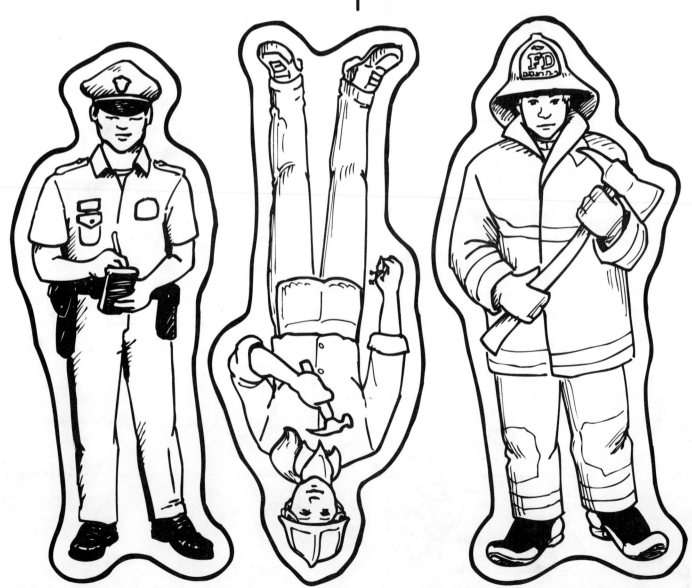

Pictures for Community Helpers

People

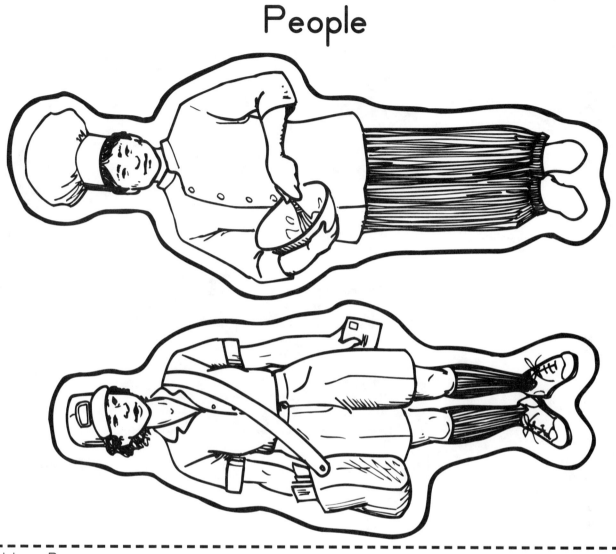

Helping Page

police
officer

construction
worker

firefighter

mail
carrier

chef

Is This My Valentine?

By

My valentine has a  on it.

Is this my valentine?

__ this my valentine?

Is ____ my valentine?

Is this __ valentine?

My valentine has a  on it.

Glue flap here.

Is this my valentine?

Glue flap here.

__ this my valentine?

Glue flap here.

Is _____ my valentine?

Glue flap here.

Is this __ valentine?

♥♥♥♥♥♥♥♥♥♥♥♥♥♥♥♥♥♥♥♥♥♥♥♥♥♥♥♥♥♥♥♥♥♥♥♥♥♥

My valentine has a  on it.

Glue flap here.

Is this my valentine?

Glue flap here.

__ this my valentine?

Glue flap here.

Is _____ my valentine?

Glue flap here.

Is this __ valentine?

3

♥♥♥♥♥♥♥♥♥♥♥♥♥♥♥♥♥♥♥♥♥♥♥♥♥♥♥♥♥♥♥♥♥♥♥♥♥♥

My valentine has a  on it.

Glue flap here.

Is this my valentine?

Glue flap here.

__ this my valentine?

Glue flap here.

Is _____ my valentine?

Glue flap here.

Is this __ valentine?

♥♥♥♥♥♥♥♥♥♥♥♥♥♥♥♥♥♥♥♥♥♥♥♥♥♥♥♥♥♥♥♥♥♥♥♥♥♥

"This is my valentine,"

said _____.

5

Pictures for Is This My Valentine?

Use for page 1	Use for page 2	Use for page 3	Use for page 4
(heart with bow)	(heart with flowers)	(heart with flowers)	I Love You
(heart with flowers)	Be My Valentine	(heart with bow)	Be Mine
(heart with tulips)	(heart with tulips)	Be Mine	Be My Valentine
Hi Cutie!	(heart with bow)	(heart with tulips)	Hi Cutie!

Where Do You Live?

By

© Instructional Fair • TS Denison

101

Do you live here?

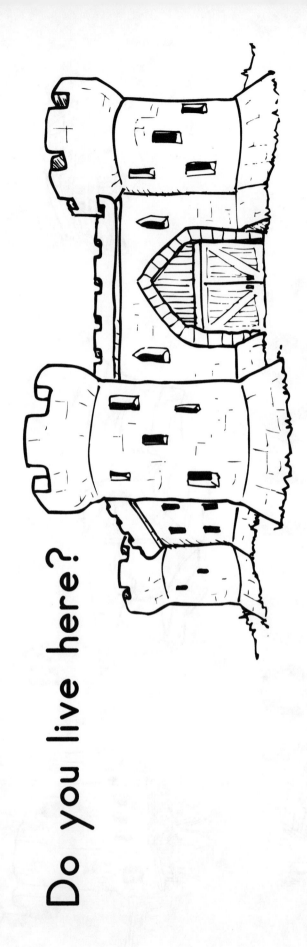

(picture of child)

Do you live here?

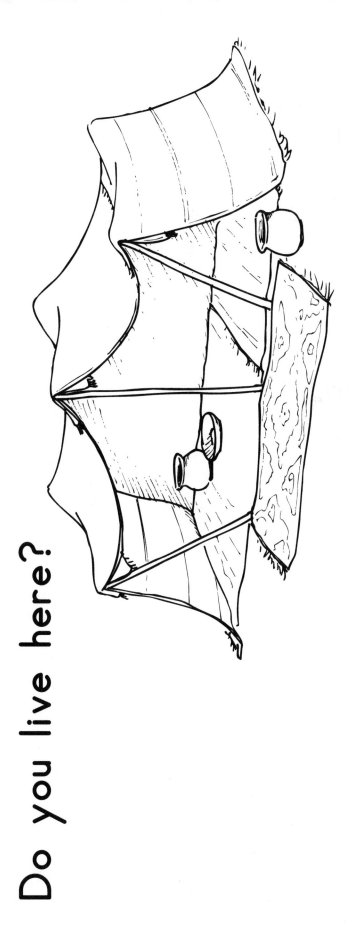

(picture of child)

Do you live here?

(picture of child)

Do you live here?

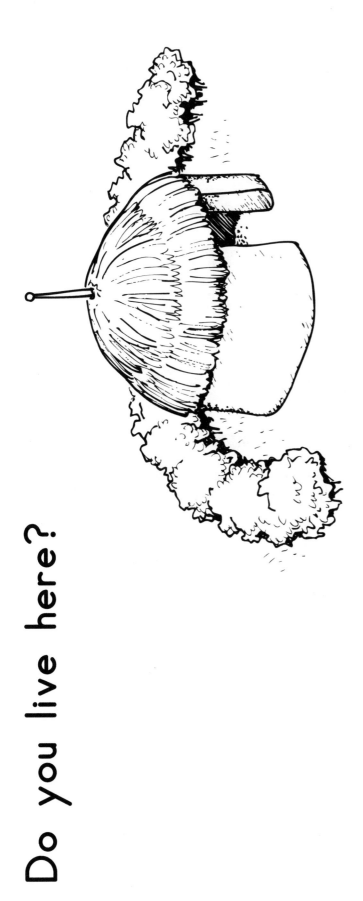

(picture of child)

© Instructional Fair • TS Denison

105

Do you live here?

(picture of child)

5

Where Do You Live?

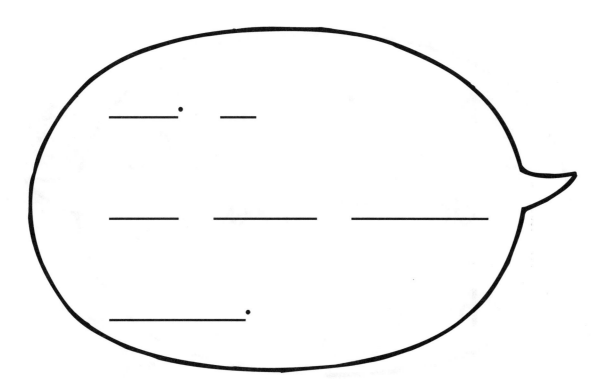

No. I do not live here.

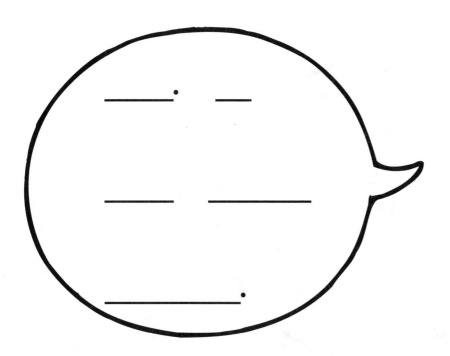

Yes. I do live here.

Where Do You Live?

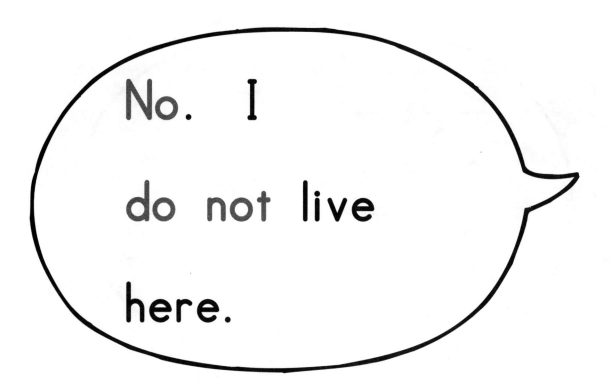

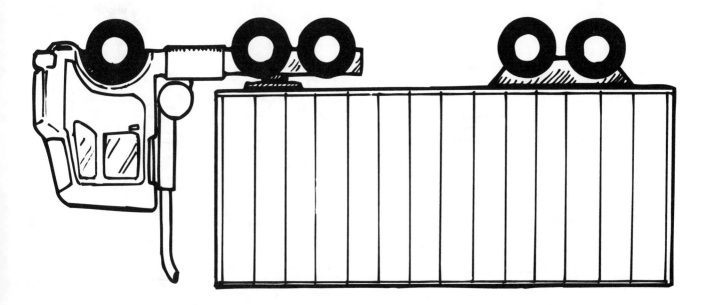

This book belongs to

Ways to Go

© Instructional Fair • TS Denison

IF21840 *Think, Do & Read*

The _lue _ar _an

_elp _e _o.

_____

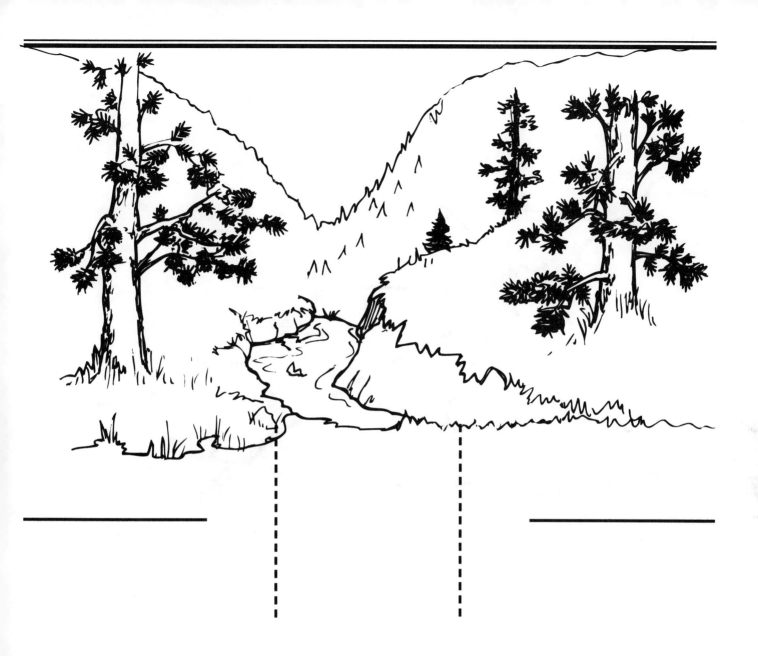

_____   _____

The _reen _eep _an

_elp _e _o.

© Instructional Fair • TS Denison

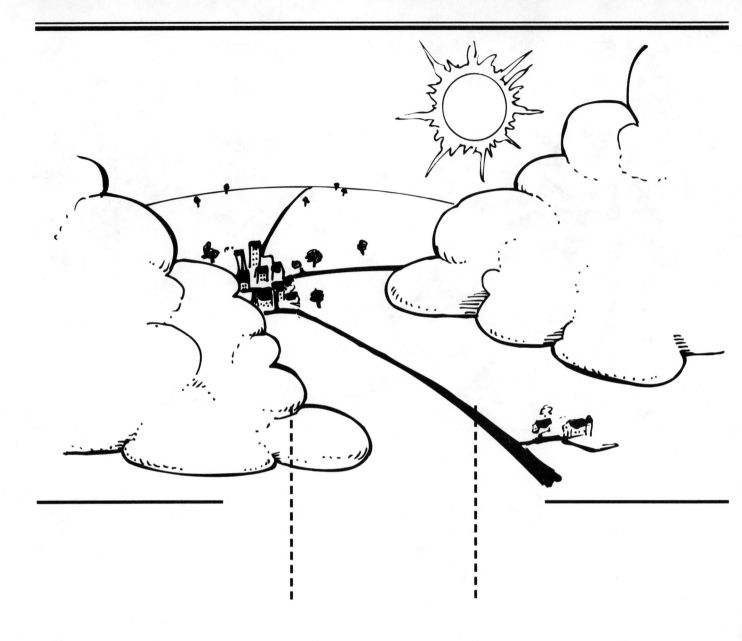

The _hite and _rey

_et _an _elp _e _o.

© Instructional Fair • TS Denison

IF21840 *Think, Do & Read*

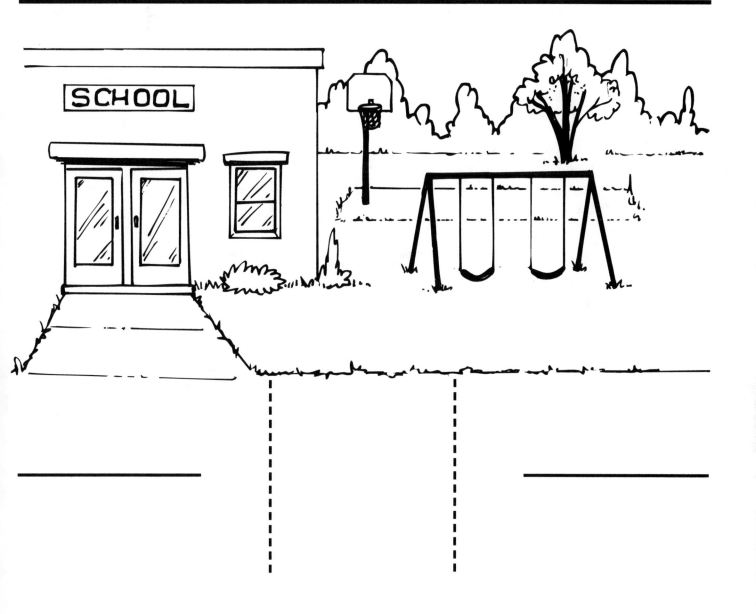

The _ellow _us _an
_elp _e _o.

© Instructional Fair • TS Denison

The _ed and _urple

_alloon _an _elp _e _o.

© Instructional Fair • TS Denison

IF21840 Think, Do & Read

My _eet _an

_elp _e _o.

© Instructional Fair • TS Denison

The _____

_an _elp _e _o.

Ways to Go

The blue car can help me go.

The green jeep can help me go.

The white and grey jet can
help me go.

The yellow bus can help me go.

The red and purple balloon can
help me go.

My feet can help me go.

© Instructional Fair • TS Denison IF21840 *Think, Do & Read*

Pictures for Ways to Go

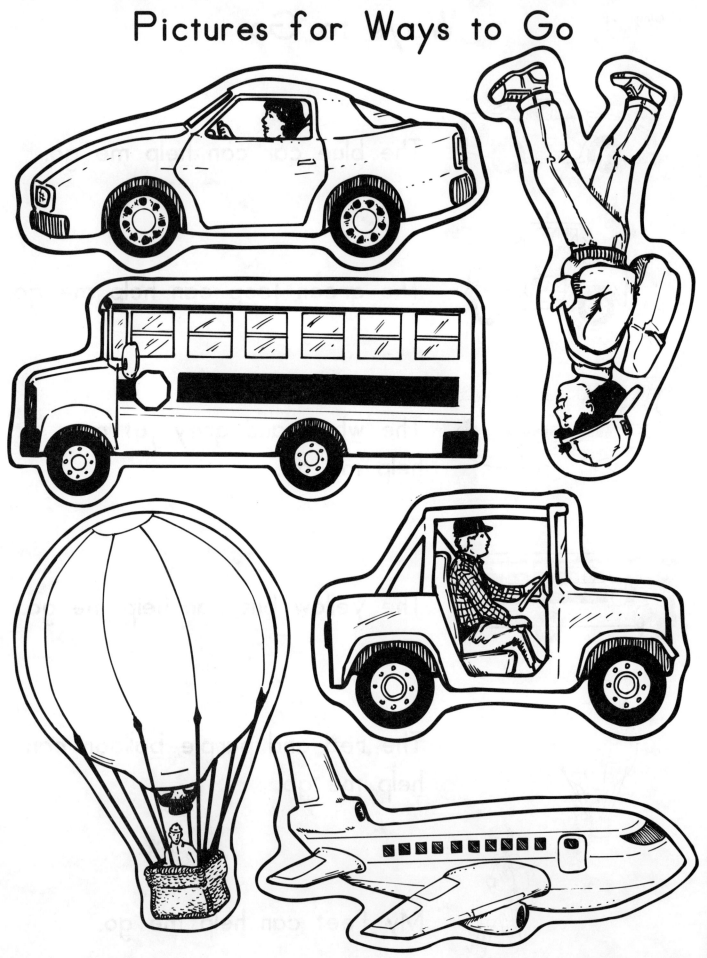

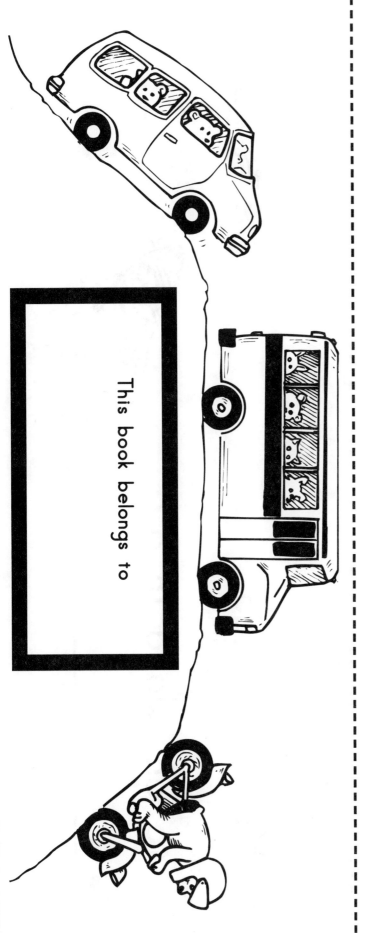

This book belongs to

Going to an Island

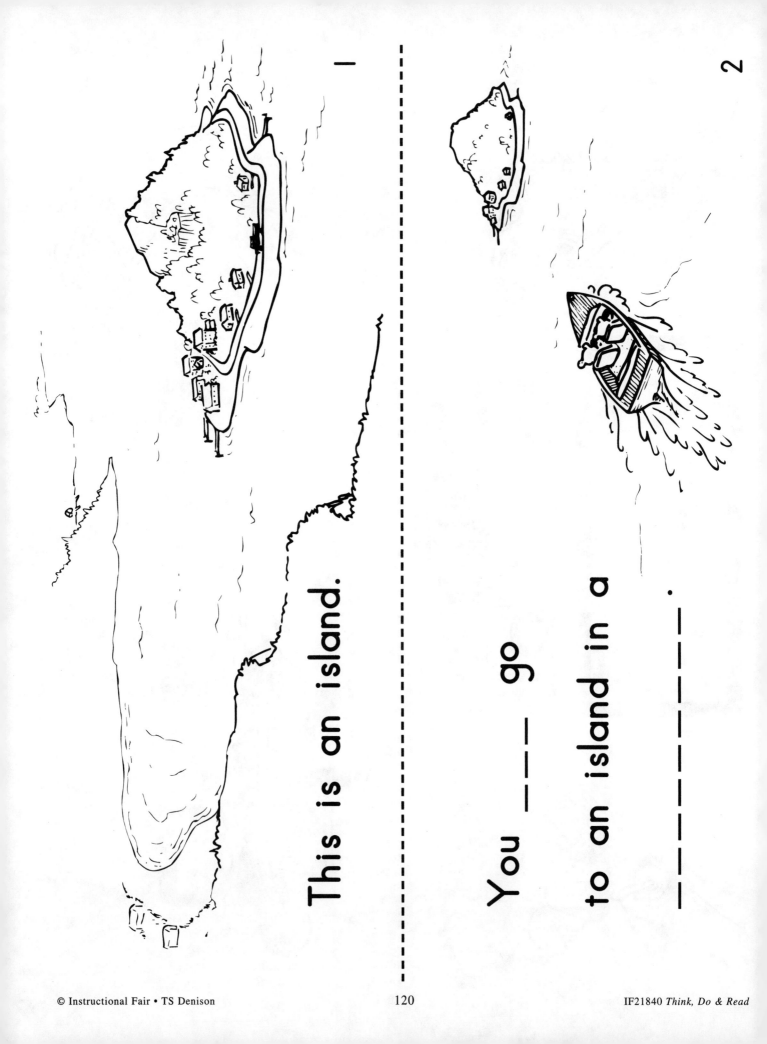

1

This is an island.

2

You _____ go

to an island in a _____ .

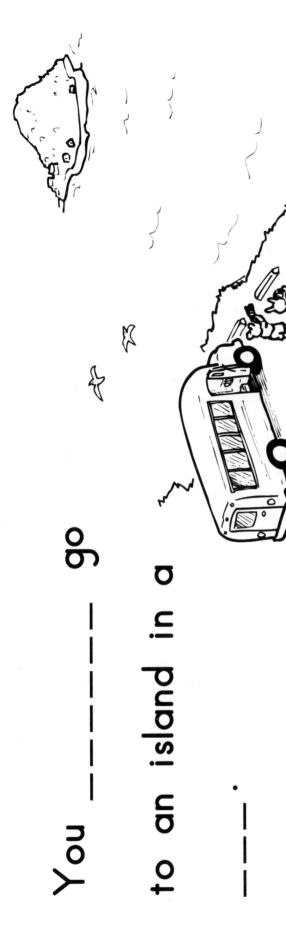

You _ _ _ go

to an island in a

_ _ _ .

You _ _ go

to an island in a

_ _ _ .

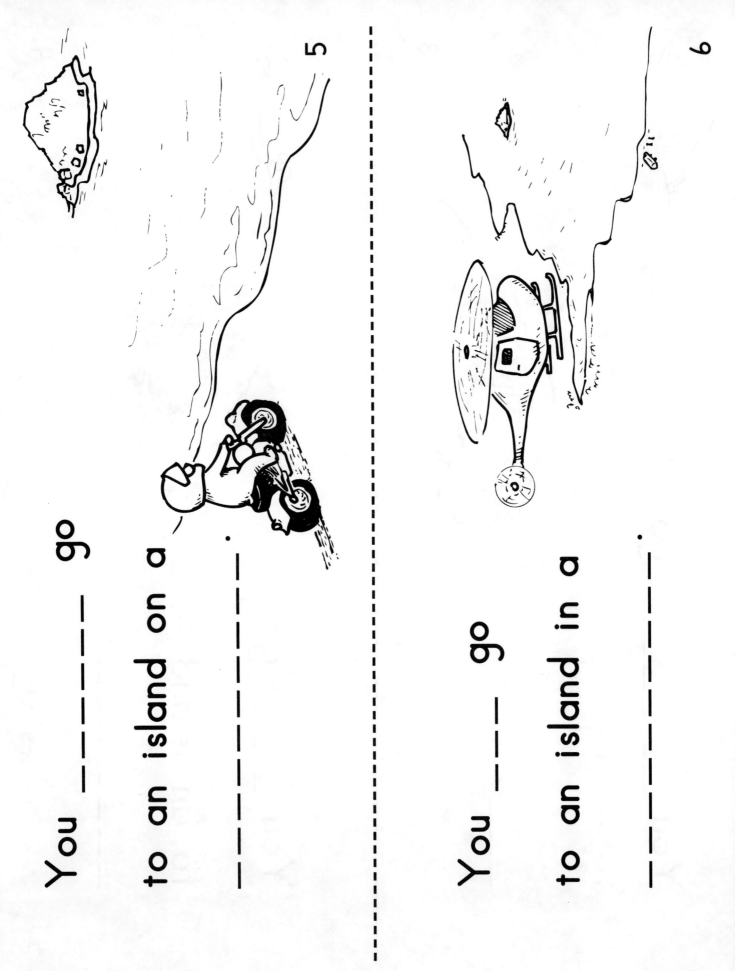

5

You _____ go

to an island on a _____.

6

You _____ go

to an island in a _____.

© Instructional Fair • TS Denison

IF21840 *Think, Do & Read*

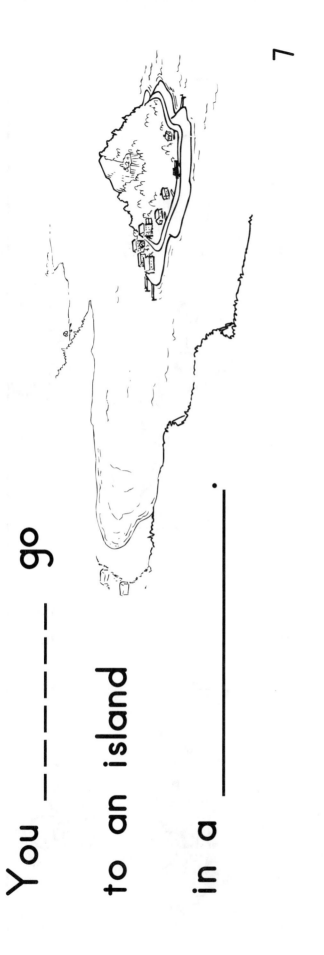

You ----- go

to an island

in a ____.

8

You ----- go

to an island in a ____.

Going to an Island

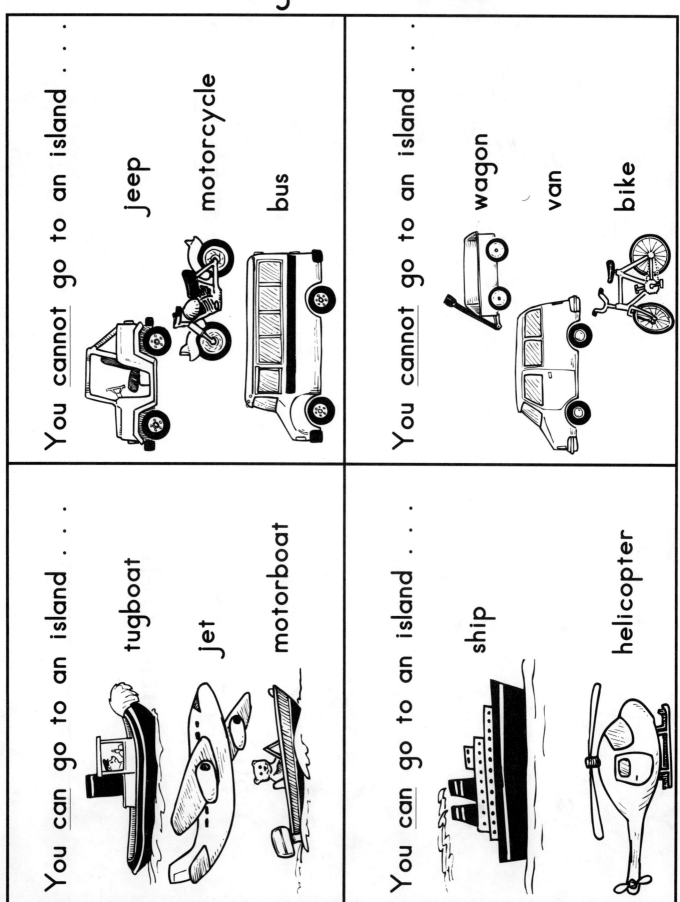

You cannot go to an island . . .

jeep

motorcycle

bus

You cannot go to an island . . .

wagon

van

bike

You can go to an island . . .

tugboat

jet

motorboat

You can go to an island . . .

ship

helicopter

The Koala

By

Here is the

island of

(1)

.

Here is the   (2)

that grows on the

island of

(1)

.

2

Here are the   (3)

that climb up the   (2)

that grows on the

island of

(1)

.

© Instructional Fair • TS Denison

IF21840 *Think, Do & Read*

3

Here is the   (4)

that has the   (3)

that climbs the   (2)

that grows on the

island of   (1)

    4

Pictures for The Koala

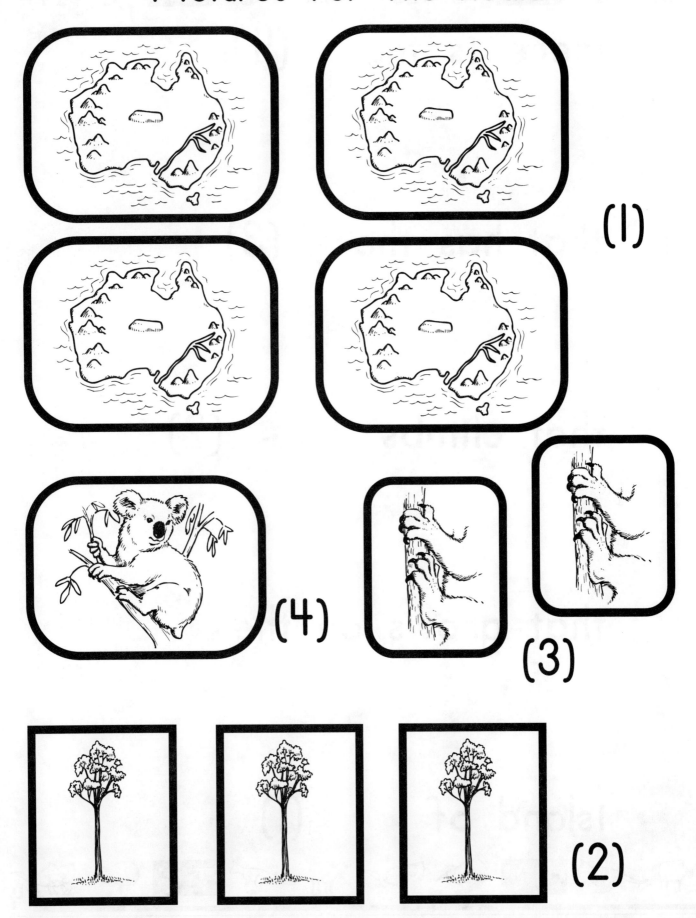

(1)

(4)

(3)

(2)

Looking for Mammals

© Instructional Fair • TS Denison

IF21840 *Think, Do & Read*

"I am looking

for a <u>mammal</u>,"

said the

"

Are you a

— — — — — — ?"

"———," said

the .

"I am a ———."

© Instructional Fair • TS Denison

133

3

"I am looking

for a mammal,"

said the

"Are you a

_ _ _ _ _ ?"

4

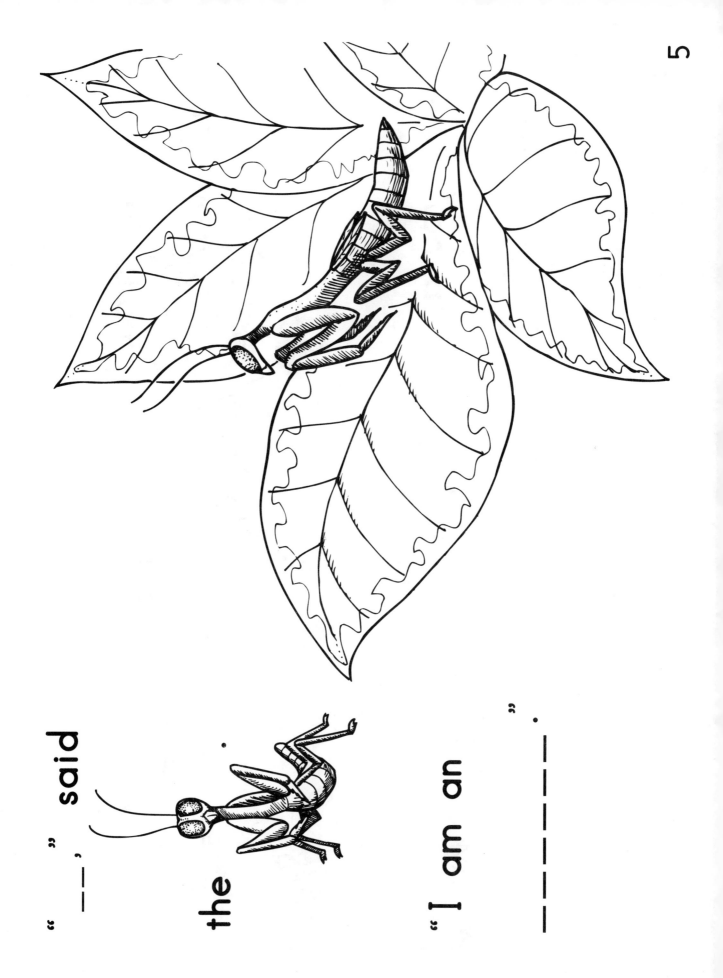

"_ _ _ _," said

the

"I am an _ _ _ _ _ _."

5

"I am looking

for a mammal,"

said the _____ .

"Are you a

__ __ __ __ ?"

6

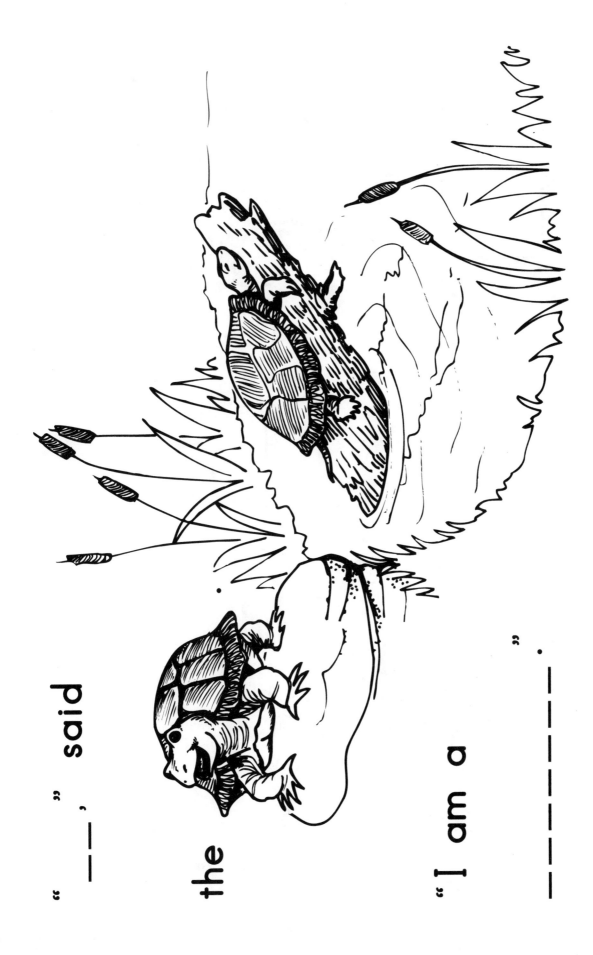

"_____," said

the

"I am a

_____."

© Instructional Fair • TS Denison

137

"I am looking

for a _mammal_,"

said the

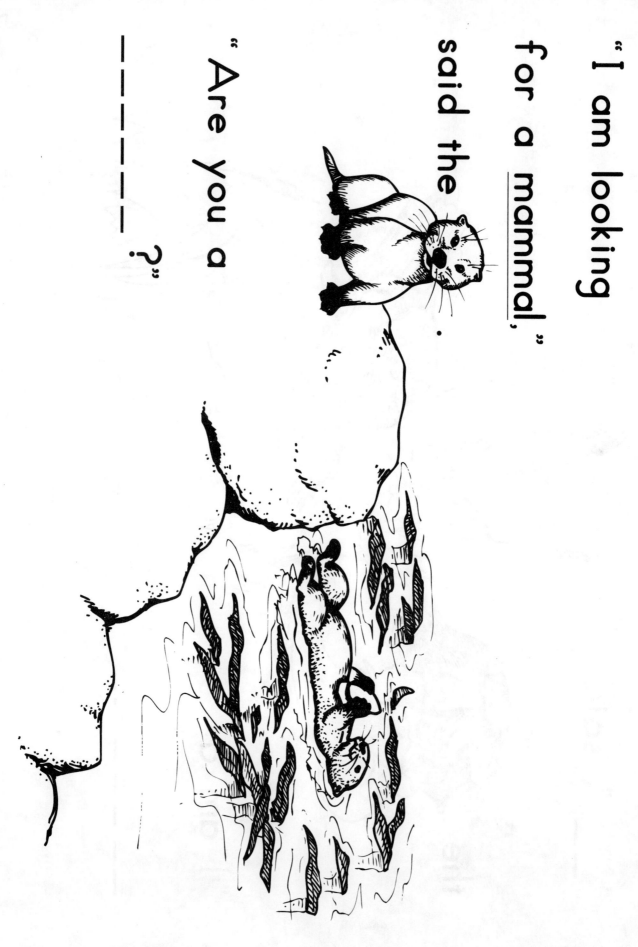

"Are you a

_ _ _ _ _ ?"

8

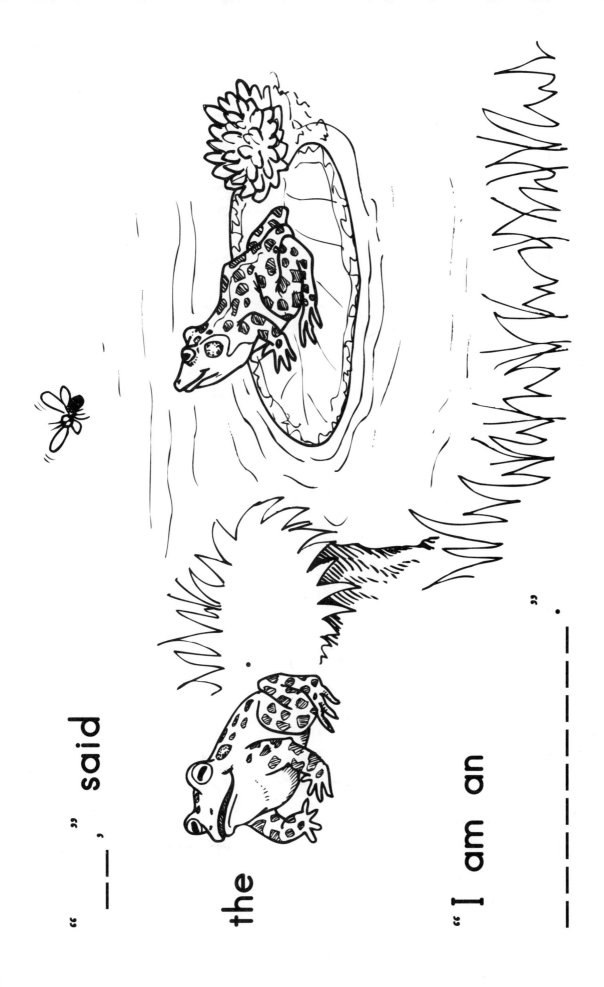

" _____ ," said

the ___.

"I am an _____ ."

9

"I am looking
for a <u>mammal</u>,"
said the

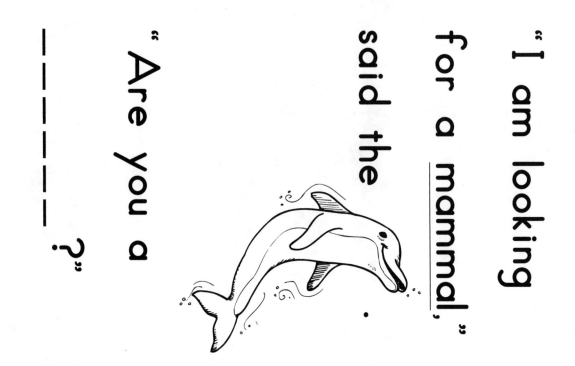

"Are you a
_ _ _ _ _ ?"

10

© Instructional Fair • TS Denison

IF21840 *Think, Do & Read*

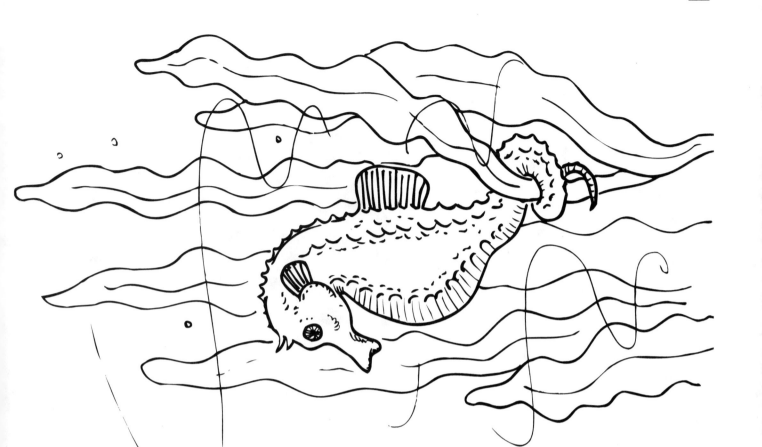

"_____," said the

"I am a _____."

"I am looking

for a <u>mammal</u>,"

said the

"Are you a

_ _ _ _ _ ?"

© Instructional Fair • TS Denison

IF21840 *Think, Do & Read*

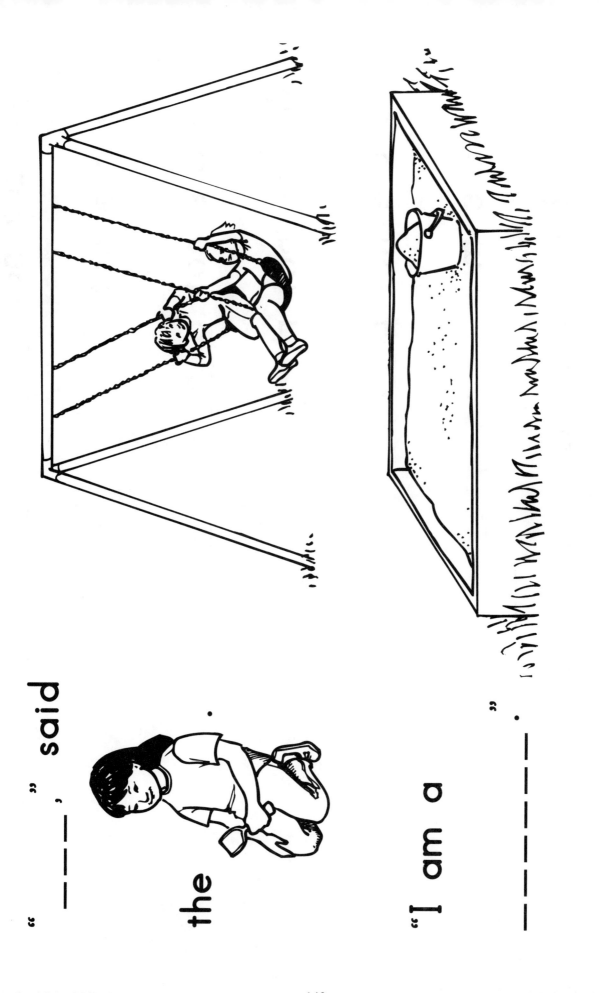

" _____ ," said

the _____ .

"I am a _____ ."

"We are not i _____.

We are not f _____.

We are not a _____.

We are not r _____.

We are not b _____.

We are m _____,"

said all the mammals together.

14

© Instructional Fair • TS Denison
IF21840 *Think, Do & Read*

We are not mammals
but we are animals.

16

I am a
praying mantis.
I am an insect.

I am a
seahorse.
I am a fish.

© Instructional Fair • TS Denison

IF21840 *Think, Do & Read*

I am a frog.
I am an
amphibian.

I am a turtle.
I am a reptile.

I am a
penguin.
I am a bird.

Looking for Mammals

Use these words:

insect   reptile

fish   bird

amphibian   mammal

Use these pictures:

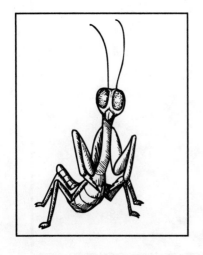

What is an amphibian?

1. It does not have <u>scales</u>.
2. It lives part of its life in the <u>water</u>.

Amphibians

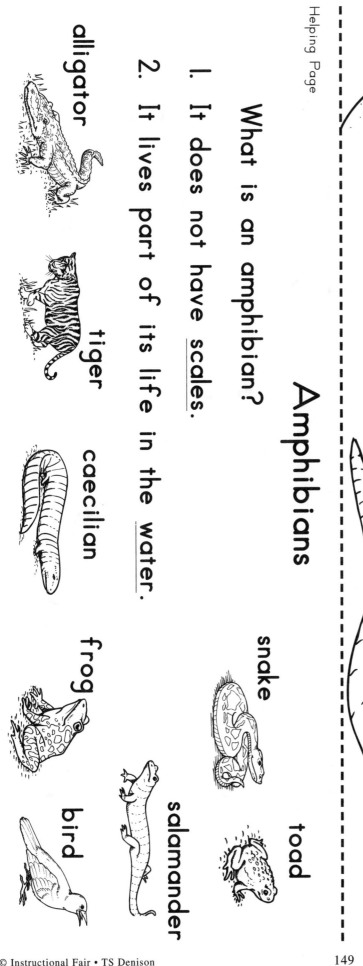

alligator

tiger

caecilian

snake

toad

salamander

frog

bird

Amphibians

By

© Instructional Fair • TS Denison

IF21840 *Think, Do & Read*

What is an amphibian?

1. It does not have ___ ___ ___.

2. It lives part of its life in the ___ ___ ___.

"I am," said the _____ .   toad

"I am not," said the _____   alligator

© Instructional Fair • TS Denison

IF21840 *Think, Do & Read*

2

"I am," said the caecilian.

"I am not," said the tiger.

"I am," said the frog.

"I am not," said the snake.

5

"I am," said the

salamander .

"I am not," said the

bird .

- - - - - - - - - - - - - - - -

6

"We are amphibians," said the animals.

f

c

s

t

© Instructional Fair • TS Denison

IF21840 *Think, Do & Read*

Pictures for Amphibians

alligator

frog

tiger

caecilian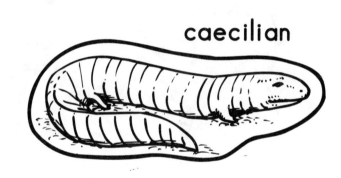

snake

toad

bird

salamander

The Little Seed

By _____

© Instructional Fair • TS Denison

IF21840 *Think, Do & Read*

"Will I grow?"
wondered the little _____.

seed

"You will need my help,"
said the brown e _____.

seed

earth

3

"Will I grow now?"
wondered the little

_____ as it snuggled into the

brown e_____.

seed

earth

4

"You will need my help,"

said the bright s____.

sun

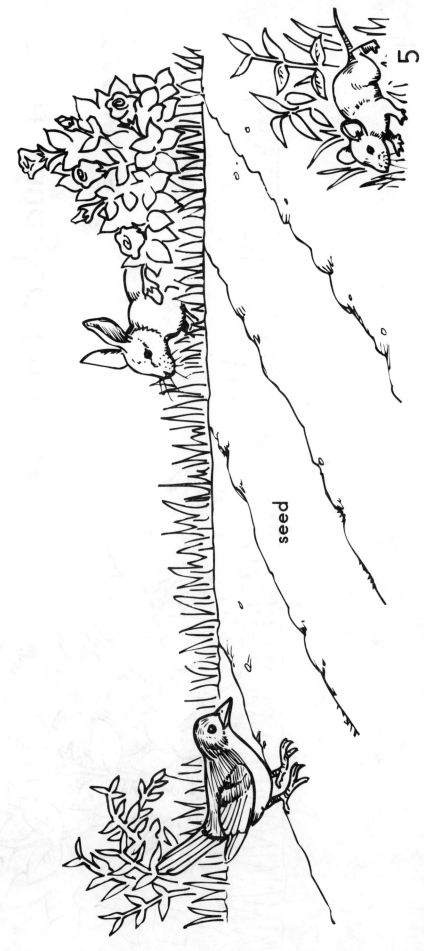

seed

5

© Instructional Fair • TS Denison

IF21840 *Think, Do & Read*

"Will I grow now?"

wondered the little _____

as it felt the bright s_____

warm the brown e_____.

sun

earth

seed

"You will need my help," said

the wet r _____ .

rain

seed

© Instructional Fair • TS Denison

IF21840 *Think, Do & Read*

"Will I grow now?"
wondered the little

_____

as it felt the wet r _____

sprinkle the warm brown e _____ .

seed

earth

"Yes! You will grown now,"

said

the e _____ and

the s _____ and

the r _____.

So the little

_____

grew,

_____

10

© Instructional Fair • TS Denison

IF21840 *Think, Do & Read*

And grew.

=

164

And grew,
until it became
a beautiful . . . .

12

© Instructional Fair • TS Denison

IF21840 *Think, Do & Read*

flower

f

© Instructional Fair • TS Denison

IF21840 *Think, Do & Read*

"Thank you

e ____, s ____,

and r ____,"

said the flower.

flower

14

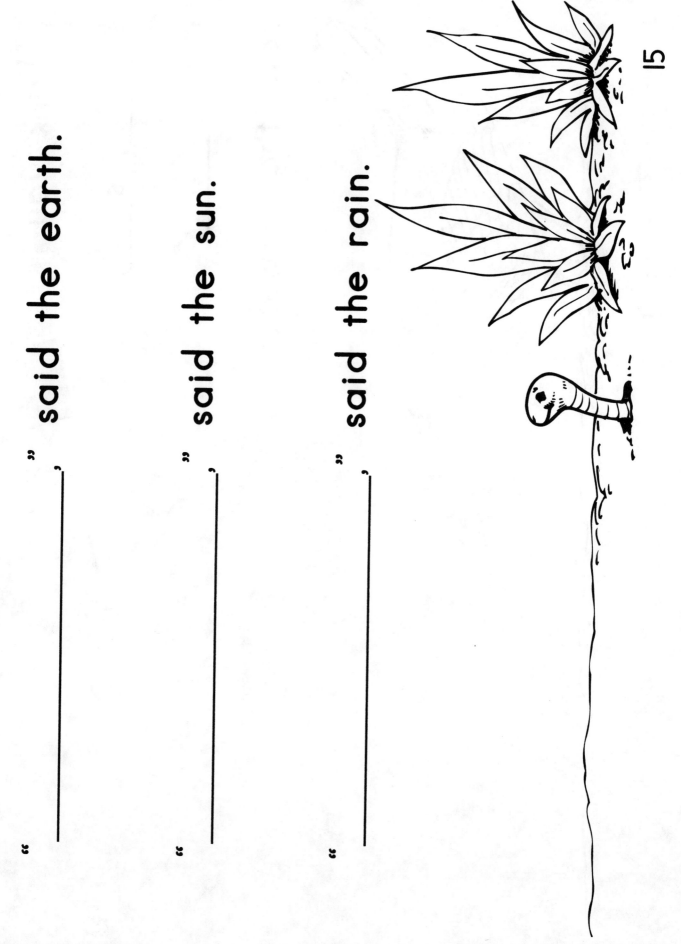

," said the earth.

," said the sun.

," said the rain.

15

© Instructional Fair • TS Denison

IF21840 *Think, Do & Read*

The Meat Eater Is Coming!

By

© Instructional Fair • TS Denison

IF21840 *Think, Do & Read*

The _teranodon saw a _yrannosaurus coming. "I will tell the other dinosaurs," she said.

X

I

"The meat eater is coming. Run!"
said the _ teranodon to the
_ rnithomimus.

✕

"The meat eater is coming. Run!" said the _rnithomimus to the _riceratops.

© Instructional Fair • TS Denison

IF21840 *Think, Do & Read*

X

"The meat eater is coming. Run!" said the _riceratops to the _orythosaurus.

4

X

"The meat eater is coming. Run!"
said the _orythosaurus to the
_yrannosaurus.

5

"But, I AM the meat eater," said the _yrannosaurus.

6

Pictures for The Meat Eater Is Coming

triceratops

corythosaurus

ornithomimus

tyrannosaurus

tyrannosaurus

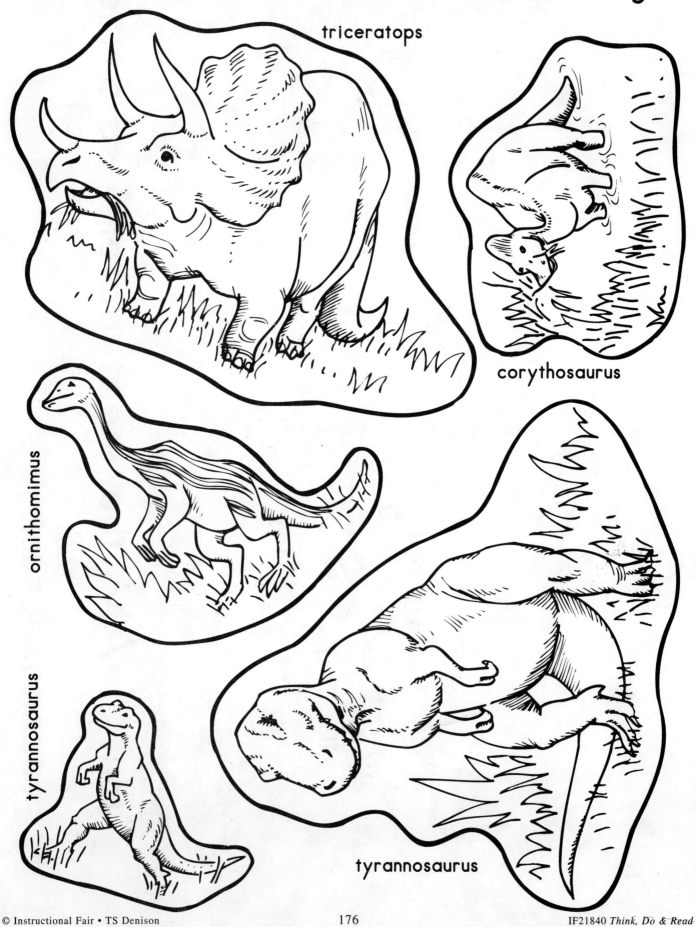